SEAMLESS SUCCESSION

SIMPLIFYING CHURCH LEADERSHIP TRANSITIONS

DR. JAY PASSAVANT

To Amy, David and Jonathan who carried the weight of being PK's throughout their teenage years and beyond with strength, integrity and faithfulness. You are still my "best references."

and

To, my wife, Carol; the mom of these three great kids and the only person that I know that could have sustained a loving and supportive home base for the 35+ years of ministry we have shared together. You deserve more than I could ever give...

TABLE OF CONTENTS

Foreward by Jim Tomberlin ix
Introduction xv
      Our Victory, His Glory
      The Seven Principles
Chapter 1: Initiate 23
      Initiate Deep Change
      Form a Transition Team
      Establish a Prayer Team
Chapter 2: Cultivate 33
      Reactive vs. Proactive
      Cultivate the Soil
      Involve Multiple Voices
Chapter 3: Communicate 42
      Engage Their Trust
      Invite the Individual
      A Tale of Poor Communication
      Logistics of Communication
      Establishing New Relationships
Chapter 4: Investigate 53
      Assess the Need
      Draft a Description
      Interviewing In-house
      Broadening to External Candidates
Chapter 5: Integrate 63
      Integrating an In-house Candidate
      Integrating an External Candidate
      Models of Integration

Chapter 6: Celebrate 73
    Continue the Genesis Rhythm
    Build a Corporate Altar
    Areas of Celebration
        Departing Pastor
        History
        New Lead Pastor
Chapter 7: Evaluate 84
    Small Change, Big Impact
    Freshman Year
    Logistics
    Identify Red Flags
Conclusion 97
Acknowledgements 101
About Passavant Leadership Group 103
End Notes 105

FOREWARD

"It isn't the changes that do you in, it's the transitions." **William Bridges**

One of the most important things a pastor needs to do in their ministry is to *finish well*.

Like death and taxes, senior pastor transition is inevitable. All pastors are interim. Pastors will be remembered more for how they left their church than how they arrived or even what they accomplished while serving it. Leave well and all the good accomplished during those years will be celebrated for years after the pastor has departed. Leave poorly and most will be forgotten. A bad transition will tarnish or erase all the good done during the years of service. The tragedy is that most pastors have not intentionally thought about how to transition well. Now they have permission and help on how to do it.

Pastor succession has been a neglected topic in the church but it is finally coming out of the closet.

The majority of churches today are led by aging baby-boomers. There is a tsunami of senior pastoral transitions coming over the next decade as these aging baby-boomers retire. Most will not be ready out of fear or uncertainty on how to start the succession conversation. Bill Hybels opened the door for public discussion of succession at Willow Creek's Leadership Summit in 2012. Then Warren Bird & William Vanderbloemen pushed the succession door wide-open in 2014 with their seminal book *Next: Pastoral Successions That Work*. Their well-researched and documentation of good, bad and ugly pastoral transitions reinforced the need for road maps towards seamless successions. Jay Passavant, who was featured in *Next,* is one of those stories. He tells it frankly in *Seamless Succession: Simplifying Church Leadership Transitions*.

I met Jay when he brought me in to help North Way Christian Church with their multisite strategy. As in so many consultations that begin with multisite, my coaching often moves into other areas of local church ministry. Having been a pastor for 25 years allows me to become a trusted friend to pastors because I have *been there, done that*. Our relationship evolved from client to friend. North Way was recovering from a bad succession attempt that got a little ugly. I had a front row seat of how Jay handled that transition, recovered from it and led the church to a good succession outcome. The church that Jay had started and grown continues to grow and flourish post-transition because of Jay's leadership towards a *Seamless Succession*.

Every senior pastoral succession is unique.

Every senior pastoral succession has its distinctive challenges and opportunities, but every senior pastor succession has to wrestle with the same issues—the departing pastor, the congregation, the staff and the new pastor. Though there is not a one-size fits all formula on how to do senior pastor transition, Jay shares seven guiding principles to help church leaders navigate toward a *Seamless Succession*.

All senior pastors are going to have a transition.

Most senior pastors choose to ignore one of the most important decisions of their ministry. Smart senior pastors plan for it. They put as much thought into how they will leave as how they started or arrived. That's what smart senior pastors do who love their congregations. This is one the most important defining moments of a senior pastor's ministry. Don't drop this ball, don't transition poorly, finish strong. *Seamless Succession* will help you do just that.

Jim Tomberlin
Founder of MultiSite Solutions
Author, 125 Tips for Multisite Churches, Better Together, and Church Locality

PREFACE

This was not going as planned. For about two years, I had been taking the initial steps of identifying and seeking to mentor a dynamic, gifted, young pastoral leader who, at some point, might become the successor to the founding pastor of North Way Christian Community.

By the grace of God, I had been honored to hold that position of founding/senior pastor of this dynamic, biblically sound, spiritually balanced body of believers in the North Hills of Pittsburgh, Pennsylvania, for over 25 years. It was very clear to me that my time of primary leadership was to come to a close so that the next generation of leaders could emerge. Success equals succession was a phrase not lost on me. Now, I had to face the reality that there was not unity or peace around this direction.

One of the characteristics that had marked our church for the entire tenure of my ministry was a very low turnover rate of pastoral leadership. This was due, in large part, to the fact that we embraced a strong *relational* component to our ministry from the highest levels of responsibility, all the way to the first time visitor. This relational component was not simply based on some emphasis that we had observed elsewhere; rather it was born of an extensive and prayerful study of most of the New Testament scriptures that were meant to describe or define what the church *should* be like.

In fact, one of the primary motivations for launching a new, non-denominational congregation, was to have the opportunity to establish a relevant, contemporary church in the 21st-century that could look and operate like the New Testament church did back in the first century. By any kind of objective study, it was clear from the New Testament Scriptures that the church was a living organism.

The Apostle Paul even described the church by using the physical human body as an illustration of how we are to work together (1 Corinthians 12).

Now, here we were, facing the first indications that perhaps the pastor we were considering was not yet prepared for this position. Rumblings were beginning to be felt, at least among the leadership level of church members, who were aware of what was going on.

What started out as a very well-intended and relaxed process of succession was beginning to look like it could cause considerable confusion, anger, and perhaps even brokenness in our beloved church family.

After a couple of months of trying to reconfigure the process, it became painfully clear that we were not on the right path and that a change had to be made. Thankfully, because of the favor of God and the wisdom of humble men and women who were in roles of leadership, we were able to bring closure to that circumstance, with some bruising, but no fracturing or permanent damage of the Body of believers.

I wanted to start *Seamless Succession* with that very brief summary so that those of you who read what follows know that I understand what's at stake here. I know how easily even well intended, mature believers can fall off of the pathway of healthy succession. I thought I was doing things well, when in fact, most of the responsibility for the pain that was caused rested on my shoulders. I needed forgiveness; and then something really awesome could begin to develop.

That is indeed what took place with the group of dedicated leaders and me who sought to do succession in a better way. What followed over the next couple of years was truly a God honoring and unity building experience that has allowed North Way and the nearly 5,000 men, women, and children who call this their church home to be thankful for their past and excited about their future!

My approach in writing *Seamless Succession* was to make it as clear and transferable as possible so that no matter whether you are a pastor, board member or in another role of influential leadership, you can use these principles as lights in a harbor that help boats or ships navigate their way to their destination.

There are only a handful of other books available on this topic, and fewer still written from the perspective of someone who has been through the experience. My prayer is that you will learn from my mistakes, as well as the principles that I share, so that your legacy might be one of a *seamless succession.*

INTRODUCTION

Our Victory, His Glory

In every life there are a handful of moments that stand apart, bumps on an otherwise smooth surface. Though nothing changes at a seismic level, though the earth still spins on its same happy tilt, these moments alter us in deep places. We are arrested, undone, remade. In a way these moments become our own "Moses moments"—we feel the burning heat of the bush, the glorious gravity of heaven bearing down on earth. We yield to the unrelenting pursuit of God drawing us near; we cease our hurrying and let our feet sink into the hallowed ground beneath us. Every fiber of our being becomes acutely aware of the Living God in our midst; our soul is drawn to its knees. The ancient Celtics called these experiences "thin places," moments where the seam between our world and the next wanes thin. There's almost a palpable holiness to them.

Like Moses, these experiences have the potential to be the origin of an entirely new trajectory; the sheer force of it all can set something in motion that influences the rest of our days. My succession was one of these burning bush moments, bringing me face to face with our God and with a specific plight of His people. Having witnessed multiple succession failures over the years in a few churches near and dear to my heart, a burden began to grow within me. There is no "gentle" failing with succession; the loss reverberates and brings havoc to pastors and church members alike. Witnessing these wrenching losses while on the inevitable journey toward my own succession event at North Way after over three decades of leading and loving my church only proved to accelerate this burden.

As you will discover in the chapters to follow, God, by his Spirit, carved out for our church, a plan to follow through the entire succession process. The outcome of this succession journey was everything that I prayed it could be. We had a new leader, the other pastors were affirmed, and my wife, Carol, and I were embraced by the church and invited to stay on as members of the team.

The Lord had proven faithful to hear my desperate cries for his wisdom and favor, taking us on this journey from an early misstep (as described in the preface) to a much different place. We came to experience a unified, celebrated and affirmed transition of leadership from the founding pastor of 30 years (me) to the man that God had in mind to lead us forward into the next season of fruitful ministry.

This transition was remarkable in its outcome because very few families left the church. In fact, many others joined as it became clear that North Way's future was not about one man's calling or singular importance. It wasn't about me, rather it was indeed God's anointing on an entire leadership team and a mature and teachable congregation. The question then became, was there anything else that I was supposed to do with this material that might be of encouragement to others on the succession journey?

The answer to that question was the result of a very striking conversation that I had with Brad Lomenick, formerly the President of Catalyst who had come to our city as a primary speaker that I had invited to a leadership conference. Through his interactions and conversations with other North Way leaders, Brad had sensed a very healthy transition was taking place. After the event, I drove Brad to the airport. As we pulled up to the 'Departing Flights' level of the greater Pittsburgh airport, Brad paused for a moment and looked directly at me and said "Jay, you have to tell this story. You have to share what you've experienced here. It could be of great encouragement to others who may be facing similar, challenging leadership transitions." Brad and I had not talked about any plans for me to write or publish on this topic. It was just on his heart as an experienced leader who has seen first-hand the painful setbacks of poor succession.

At that very moment, I knew that the Lord was speaking through Brad to me that I was to write the essence of this experience in some sort of publication that could be widely viewed by anyone, of any size church, with the potential of encouraging them to believe for outstanding outcomes and healthy transitions.

What follows are not simply the words of a theorist or someone who has studied numerous leadership transitions. Though I value those insights, there are things that are learned by going *through the process* that cannot be learned any other way. I have endeavored to share the emotions, heartaches, sacredness, and joy of the succession journey as I experienced it. Now, well over three years later, North Way, a multi-site church of five campuses, along with a world missions commitment in 20 nations, is thriving in every sense of the word. God has been good to us!

Never were the words of Paul, writing to the Church in Corinth, more appropriate than when it comes to these matters of succession and transition: "If one part suffers, every part suffers with it; if one part is honored, every part rejoices with it." (1 Cor.12:26)

My hope in writing this book is that it will serve to provide a bit of a vaccination from the succession/transition virus. For those already afflicted, perhaps it will serve as a possible antidote to reverse the infection.

We live in a day when tens of thousands of churches are facing the likelihood of a change in senior leadership over the next several years. In what may be the most critical decision a local church will ever face, my desire is that these words, written from the flesh and blood of my own church's life, will come alongside the Living Word and contribute to the possibility that every church can remain healthy from one generation to the next.

This expresses in a tangible way the essence of our vision statement at North Way: "One church, multiple locations, all generations."

In all of my research leading up to succession, and even during succession, I rarely came across material that gave adequate attention to both the gravity and the glory of the succession process. There was little, if any, reference to the aim and hope of God for His people through this process. I did, however, find a plethora of material that erred towards either pessimism and fear, or pride and naiveté. All of which, in their own way, are indicative of a less than God-centered approach to succession, meaning one that takes into account His power and presence. Even a cursory look through the Bible will leave you with the unmistakable impression that God is always beautifully involved in matters that affect the growth and unity of His people. Would it not then be safe to draw the conclusion that if a failed succession attempt has the possibility of causing damage to the Body of Christ that this is a matter of great concern to our God?

In their excellent book on this topic, William Vanderbloemen and Warren Bird say, "…we examined almost two hundred case studies of high-visibility successions, including some of the best and worst. We conducted more than fifty extended interviews – many onsite in the pastor's office."[1] There is no doubt that this is a common place where the church can and does run into harm. Most—if not all—churches will at some point undergo a significant leadership change if they desire to continue beyond the span of one individual's leadership, making this a universal issue. As a result, succession needs to be a place where significant time, effort, and resources pull together so that instead of coming through this process battered and weakened, we work together to find our victory, and His glory.

The burning bush was God's invitation to Moses to participate in His work of liberating His people and expanding His Kingdom. This is still His work; His people are at the very core of all His efforts. This is the reason why my goal in approaching succession cannot— must not—be that of a scant hope of survival but the tenacious and seamless pursuit of expanding His Kingdom. When a church truly believes that at the core of this pivotal season is a good God inviting us to draw near, to take off our shoes, and stand in awe, something critical changes. I've watched it—felt it—happen. When we truly expect to encounter God, when we anticipate the plans of a good God stirring in this hallowed season, we stop fearing succession and instead welcome it as an opportunity to champion the history that God is forming for His Bride.

It is very possible to go through the whole process of succession and miss these deeper currents at work, to begin this journey with heavy foreboding instead of a sense of honor and expectation. My hope and prayer is that you would allow this book to be a place where you take off your shoes and stay awhile. You camp out. You listen. You meet with the Living God and approach this season with humble confidence, reveling in the privilege of participating in God's pursuit of His bride.

The Seven Principles

Before I address the layout of the book, I want to clarify that our use of the word "seamless" throughout these pages is not intended to be interchangeable with the word "perfect." I did not navigate this change perfectly; there was need for grace at every turn. Our congregation and leadership team, myself included, will all willingly attest to that. In fact, there are a few instances popping into my mind where we stood on the brink of failure, toes pressed to the edge of a dark crisis brewing. I use the term "seamless" to reiterate the possibility of a grace-filled, Spirit-led, God-glorifying succession process that allows for the seamless and effective pursuit of the heart and will of God both during and after the succession season. I remain convinced that "seamless" is what the Lord desires; it's our fallen nature that sometimes causes that journey to be longer than expected.

In the remainder of this book I introduce seven core principles that have emerged out of my experiences, conversations, prayer, and dialogue. Although they may not always be in this exact order, they are: initiate, cultivate, communicate, investigate, integrate, celebrate, and evaluate. I found each one to be important in terms of maintaining a disciplined but reasonable pace in making the succession experience a very positive one. I use the term "principle" because the succession process is not necessarily linear. The details of succession will vary from one church to the next, but in every succession there exists a measure of predictability, necessary momentum, and critical steps that must be given attention to before progressing. Kotter describes this well: "[T]he change process goes through a series of phases that, in total, usually require a considerable length of time. Skipping steps creates only the illusion of speed and never produces a satisfying result. A second very general lesson is that critical mistakes in any of the phases can have a devastating impact, slowing momentum and negating hard-won gains."[2]

The principles trace the natural order of my own succession process, and while the specifics of the content relate to pastoral succession, I believe that all significant transitions will be bene-fitted by these principles. The success of each principle is deter-mined by the effective navigation (or lack thereof) of the principle before it, though some overlap will always be present. I recognize that there is certainly more than one way to do succession and am only sharing what I have found to be effective and what has proven itself in the years following the transition. Many of the churches that I've studied, and people I've talked with over the past several years, would largely agree that the seven principles included in this book are commonly held by most churches (and other organizations) that have done this well.

I've given significant thought on how to frame these seven prin-ciples. Some of the concepts require more than just a quick decision. In some cases, they may represent an entire mental or spiritual par-adigm shift. It's on the specific points of application like this where a conversation with the leadership team could prove quite helpful in adapting the principles to fit the unique culture of your church. Most of these principles are valuable not just for the succession of the senior leader but can apply to transitions of other members of your team, whether in spiritual, nonprofit, or even secular environments.

At the end of each chapter I provide a series of important ques-tions and observations intended to maximize the impact of the con-tent, regardless of whether you are reading this as part of the team tasked with leading a succession, or if you just want to understand the process better yourself. I wanted to include these as an ongoing reminder throughout the book for you to sit awhile and reflect, to examine and celebrate the detailed way God is leading you in each specific stage of the journey.

My hope is for this book to help you navigate succession far beyond the timid hope of survival to a place of rich celebration in our Living God and the new leader of His Church for this season. I hope to clarify and widen the margin between failure and suc-cess, removing some of the ambiguity in the process as I go along. Succession is not meant to be a disorienting process that leaves your congregation in ruins. This is meant to be an opportunity for the life-giving Spirit of God to continue His seamless and wonderful work of building the Body and bringing it into all fullness. May this book serve and strengthen you in this pursuit of the Glory of God and the victory of His people throughout the succession process.

Blessings,
Jay Passavant

Founding Pastor
North Way Christian Community

CHAPTER 1:
INITIATE

Initiate Deep Change

I n his book *Deep Change*, Robert Quinn makes a valuable distinction between two levels of change: incremental change and what he terms "deep change."[3] Incremental change typically feels within our control. The adjustments needed are minor; we take them in stride. Incremental change may require us to work longer hours, or exert greater effort, but they usually only involve an expansion or small alteration to what we're already doing. Our territory widens. This could look like a new program added to an already existing department, or a second service scheduled to accommodate more people. In our current day this level of change is very common, both in our personal life and the life of the church. If the new change doesn't work, it's easy to regroup and try again. There's little risk involved.

A change in primary leadership, however, is not a surface or incremental change. Succession fits under the second level of change: deep change, which requires new ways of thinking, an utter break from old paradigms. Every life and every organization will experience some measure of deep change. These changes are not a mild speed bump in the midst of life; these are the changes that define us. Deep change is usually not linear. It's messy and filled with backtracking, readjustment, and prayer—and if we're wise, *lots* of prayer.

Though it may seem painfully obvious, the first step in this is to begin the conversation about succession. Avoiding the conversation does not mean avoiding the change. If a church or organization hopes to live beyond the span of one leader's service, then succession will be necessary. And if they hope to experience future seasons of growth and efficiency without any lag time between the two, then a *seamless succession* will be necessary.

Although it may seem counterintuitive, I've noticed that many leaders are reticent to discuss succession planning, even though they would almost all affirm it as an event intimately connected to the future health of their church. What is surprising is that most leaders who have been with the church for a considerable length of time wait until their desired time for transition is right around the corner before even beginning this conversation. While most mature leaders know that the day is coming, they tend to believe that it's not "quite yet" and therefore postpone initiation of the succession process, oftentimes to the point that it compromises the future of the church.

Unfortunately, in many environments starting this discussion requires a very brave soul. Congregations tend to develop a deep affection for their pastor and indeed, the pastor for his congregation. In a purely human sense, it can feel like an affront to bring up the topic as if somehow discussing a new leader is disrespectful or disloyal to the current one. And so due to an intended but tragically misplaced kindness to the current leader, the discussion is avoided to the detriment of both the church and the current leader.

If the pastor fails to initiate this conversation, and if those in position of authority, such as the board of elders, also fail to act, the process will begin with an undue and unnecessary amount of stress as a result. This is why it is so important that the senior pastor is the one to not only acknowledge that the time for change is approaching, but to also be the one to lead and champion the change emotionally and spiritually. Ideally, this process should be embraced at least three years from the anticipated time of the succession event. In fact, Pastor Rick Warren of the Saddleback Church announced many years ago that he was called to lead the church for forty years. It is very likely he is already thinking about the succession process even though it is still a few years away. In my experience and study, about three years is almost necessary to do succession well, especially if the church expects the search for candidates to extend outside its own congregation.

It's also worth noting that much of the assessing and preliminary work that is part of the process can be enormously helpful in the event of some sort of unexpected event. Recently, a very well-known pastor in our city who stays in shape and takes care of himself physically suffered a serious heart attack while on the treadmill. Thankfully, he pulled through, though his heart stopped a couple of times, as I understand it. The leadership team now has opportunity to engage in a thoughtful process for succession, but they were literally a few minutes away from losing their long-term leader without a clear plan in place. For this reason alone, it is a wise step for any healthy church or other organization to take while everything is working well. It's a sign of strength, not fear or weakness. In many ways, it's something similar to a well thought out and executed personal will.

I hope that just raising this issue will give you permission to make the topic of succession a point of open conversation long before any action may be required. If there is any possibility that you will be making a move from the role of pastoral or senior leader in the next few years, I would encourage you to initiate the conversation around a succession plan. When the lead pastor initiates the conversation, it provides a graceful invitation to others and lets them know that the topic is open for discussion. Remember that God spoke to Moses about preparing Joshua to take his place as the leader of his chosen people many decades before it happened (Numbers 27:18-21). Every leadership position will inevitably come to an end, and the leader holds the greatest power over setting the tone of beginning the transition.

Form a Transition Team

In our form of church government, a sub-grouping of the Board of Elders called the Elders' Council is responsible for all senior-level personnel decisions. Because we always sought to be as transparent as possible about staffing decisions, the Board of Elders were usually informed and even invited to pray about such decisions long before they were made by the Elders' Council.

Rather than just use the individuals on the Board of Elders who are normally responsible for this type of decision or the personnel team that had been responsible for recommendations previously, we believed that an entirely new group of people was needed for such a major event in the life of our church. We chose a broad cross-section of mature and committed people that together seemed to represent the core of our congregation. This allowed our search to be reviewed by a demographically diverse group of people who were willing to address the immediate and long-term issues until they were totally unified as it related to our future needs and vision. The people chosen had demonstrated a deep commitment to the vision and mission of the church through their personal sacrifice and service. It was the responsibility of this group, who we referred to as the "transition team" to go through the arduous task of vetting all internal candidates, as well as be prepared to interface with a highly regarded search firm if no internal candidate was found. It was not the responsibility of the transition team to select the next senior leader, but rather, to recommend one or even two candidates that they felt best aligned with the needs and culture of North Way.

Each member of the transition team was skilled at communicating openly with others and expressed an availability and willingness to enter into this intensive process. We knew that this select group of members would need to meet regularly and therefore could not be larger than eight or nine individuals. Our team consisted of several members of the congregation who were deeply involved in ministry, two members of the Elders' Council, some mature female leaders, a representative from one of the campuses, a gifted and trained human resource person, and myself as the current senior pastor. The inclusion of a few paid staff members on the team helped to streamline the communication to the congregation as the staff members had access to the necessary resources to send and receive important communications.

We were very fortunate to have a church member who was highly trained and experienced in the secular marketplace in such processes and made him the convener of the transition team. He made certain that the team had a clear weekly agenda and was faithful to meet as promised. I cannot overstate how important it is to have an objective individual on the team, even if this person is a consultant from outside of your congregation, to help you accurately perceive your own internal communications and provide you with clear support and direction along the way.

The transition team worked to formulate a strategic time line and then delegate tasks to the individual(s) best suited to each task. Because two of the nine members of the transition team were part of the Elders' Council, we knew that monthly updates would be forthcoming from the transition team to the Elders' Council. This helped establish a healthy measure of accountability and expectation. The team had the full blessing of the Elders' Council and knew that they were accountable for meeting regularly to sustain the momentum of the process and did so with a sense of privilege. So, to revisit this critical piece of the transition puzzle, the transition team was:

- demographically diverse
- comprised of staff and volunteer members
- available to keep a rigorous commitment (usually 2 hours a week)
- willing to listen to others as well as have their own areas of focus
- committed to unity more than having their own way in the final decision

The team convener would lay out a proposed agenda several days before the meeting, thus allowing us to come equipped in our thoughts and even in our expectations for a productive and fruitful meeting. Timelines were established for recognized steps in the process such as, but not limited to:

- evaluating internal candidates (more on this in the "Investigate" chapter)
- communicating relevant information with the entire congregation
- providing written updates for the Elders' Council, etc.
- allowing enough time for thoughtful processing of all input while remaining committed to a specific date of transition to a called and qualified candidate

We also knew that if no internal candidate met the necessary requirements, the process would be extended up to one year longer so that we could engage a specialized search firm to help us locate potential candidates around the country. Both the Elders' Council and

I (Jay) were in agreement about this optional extension. I am convinced that establishing a timeline is a healthy motivator in terms of getting the process going. However, we never felt bound by those dates as much as directed by them.

Convening a transition team that, for the most part, was always available to hear the heartfelt insight by any one of the members, or to give a brief, but official, update every month or so, gave the entire process a much more transparent feel. In today's culture, people want a voice in the decision being made. In a larger church it is impossible for everyone to be intimately involved in the selection and transition process details, but we wanted to honor and respect our church members by providing people and opportunities for them to express suggestions or concerns along the way. This was done through clear access on the web; social media and email, and frequent reminders that following most every worship service, at least one transition team member was available for interaction and conversation.

A baseline of confidentiality was set, but except for personal information, members were continually informed of the activities of transition team. When the people felt that this critical process was not being held in secret, but with openness and even a desire for input, it made huge deposits in the account called trust, which every leader knows is essential to accomplishing the mission. I had heard of too many cases where congregations felt disrespected because they were not offered an opportunity to be heard, and as a result it hindered, or even altogether halted, their willingness to give the future leader an honest chance to succeed. Do everything possible to avoid even the appearance of secret meetings by a small, closed group who literally hold the key to determining who is to lead a sizable community of believers going forward.

The transition team's role in the succession process is pivotal. They bear the beautiful privilege of helping the church body navigate through a difficult and multi-faceted change. Each member of the transition team understood the gravity of the decision and made an intentional effort to get to know one another so that the communication could be transparent, honest, and edifying. We knew from the beginning that the relational dynamics within the transition team were very important. These were men and women who needed to be able to put personal preferences aside for the sake of listening to what the Lord might be saying through one another. We also made use of the skills that these individuals could bring to the process. We wanted to be intentional in using the best of the natural resources we could find; proactive, engaging, experienced, intelligent; as well as the spiritual maturity that we deemed necessary to proceed with a well-balanced transition team. Looking back on it, I'm not sure if I would have qualified, given the high bar we had set.

At some point along the way, every person on the transition team was struck with the realization that the laborers with whom they were engaged might very well determine the long-term fruitfulness and blessing of the church they had grown to love. The meetings were not beset with any sense of heaviness or foreboding. Rather, there was a very clear sense of joy and anticipation as the members embraced the calling to which they had committed themselves. Could it be that this is the same spirit Paul writes of in 1 Thessalonians 2:19–20, "For what is our hope, our joy, or the crown in which we will glory in the presence of our Lord Jesus when he comes? Is it not you? Indeed, you are our glory and joy." The true joy was in the journey, not just the destination.

Establish a Prayer Team

We also understood that for this process to be effectively engaged there would need to be substantial covering of ongoing and widely embraced intercessory prayer from start to finish. Although it's not within the scope of this book to convince the reader about the importance of prayer, we believed that entering into a decision of this magnitude without a profound sense of the spiritual dynamics at work would be very naïve. As one of the great church leaders of another generation said: "[Prayer] is where the action is. Any church without a well-organized and systematic prayer program is simply operating a religious treadmill."[4]

As we stood on the brink of this season of tremendous change, we set about to identify, confirm, and empower a prayer team to undergird the actions of the transition team and all the other dynamics at play. If your team doesn't already know the statistics of failed successions, it might be of worth to share this with the foundational members. I don't suggest this as a way of fostering fear; rather, alerting them to the reality of the mission and the very real and urgent need for their faithful support. These are the people who will lift tired arms and build a hedge of greatly needed protection against things seen and unseen. Their ministry in this season is invaluable for the future of the church and its continued legacy.

Anyone who searches the historical landscape of church succession will find it covered with the most unfortunate weeds of unforeseen failure. As I've said previously, this is quite possibly the most important and strategic decision that a new or even seasoned church that has a long-standing pastor will ever face. It stands to reason that the evil one would seek to do anything within his power to cause the church to stumble and perhaps even split, or worse, break apart into multiple pieces just when the church is about ready to take its next leap of effectiveness and faith. That is why determined, consistent and very focused prayer must be embraced by a significant percentage of the congregation and most importantly, those in positions of leadership and authority. As one of the little-known but profoundly wise forefathers of the faith, S.D. Gordon said: "prayer is the battle, ministry is simply taking home the victory."[5]

The initial members of the prayer team were sought out by invitation of the elders and then joined by others who had visibly embraced that role in previous seasons of the church's life. It was truly an honor to have individuals who had demonstrated a passion for prayer for many years in the life of the church involved in this significant part of our history. After a core group had formed, we opened the prayer team meetings to all other members of the congregation who felt led to participate. Although the entire church family was encouraged to be praying about this most important transition process, it was very reassuring to know that on any given night both at the church and in homes around the area, people were meeting to pray specifically about our transition event.

The information that was given to those who were praying for us was never confidential or overly personal. We supplied enough information to promote unity of heart and to guide their prayers to be relevant and effective for the mission at hand. However, it's very fair to say that we knew that this was a significant step in securing a high level of faith and confidence in our transition process.

Though this is not something that I can prove analytically, all the members of the transition team sensed that God was going before us in the process, and very few obstacles or diversions took place along the way. I believe this can only be attributed to the significant number of people praying for us and the process, on a daily basis. E. M. Bounds sums it up beautifully: "God shapes the world by prayer. The prayers of God's saints are the capital stock of heaven by which God carries on his great work on the Earth."[6] Prayer recognized and affirmed regularly—both within our team and corporately—became an integral part of the succession process. *If I were compelled to point to just one component of the succession process that it enabled it to become a seamless event, it would be because of this mysterious, but very real sense, that God was in control because we asked Him to be, every single day in personal and corporate prayer.*

Numerous members who participated in transition prayer reported back to me that they "sensed the value of their involvement" and counted it a privilege to pray. Your responsibility is to continue to provide them with current information and to openly and frequently express appreciation for their faithfulness.

Change has now been initiated. It's now time to move on and look carefully at the second significant principle of a succession plan: Cultivate.

Discussion Questions for Chapter 1: Initiate

1. To your knowledge, does your church or organization have any kind of succession plan in place should your senior pastor/leader be called unexpectedly to leave your church/ministry? (It happens every day in a church somewhere in America). Who would be charged with the responsibility of enacting such a plan?
2. Why is a positive succession plan necessary if your church wants to be multigenerational? Explain.
3. Why is it that both pastors and church families are reluctant to talk about such planning?

4. What do you perceive the benefits of a transition team would be if your church is facing an upcoming transition? (p. 26)
5. To whom would your church leadership turn to find some assistance in establishing a transition team or some similar group of select individuals who represent most every season of life and understand your core ministries?
6. Why is having a voice important when not everyone has a vote? (p. 28-29)
7. Does your church have a significant, inclusive, and well-led prayer ministry? What might you do to see that such a group comes together around this process?

CHAPTER 2:
CULTIVATE

Reactive vs. Proactive

The characteristic of cultivation is one that should be deeply imbedded in the culture of the local church. Sadly, this is generally not the case. We spend far more time reacting to situations than we do proactively creating a healthy culture that lends itself to producing new ideas, developing leaders, and being receptive to change. Successions tend to mirror this same default: we react to the changes unearthed by succession as they come up. Granted, this approach requires less time up front. There's less planning and fewer meetings. We're able to expend a smaller amount of energy because we aren't pursuing preventative measures and, as a result, fewer resources are needed initially. Overall, in the beginning this way will *feel* easier. But what can happen as a result of this approach, especially in a succession event, is that things can—and will—quickly spiral out of control, causing us to spend months unnecessarily scrambling due to lack of preparation. It becomes a battle to restore order and joy.

I believe that, against the odds, growth and renewal are possible in this season. I believe that the will and heart of God for His people is *always* growth and life. I know that as leaders, we are responsible to cultivate the soil of our hearts so that we are prepared to glorify God and advance His Kingdom in every circumstance and every change, including succession. The purpose of this chapter on cultivation is to eradicate a few roots that have the potential to cause a great deal of *unnecessary* inefficiency and stress in your succession journey, and many times even failure. I do not believe that succession is doomed to be a graceless and frazzled undertaking, but when we go through it solely in reactionary mode, it can easily become that. Most of us have witnessed how exhaustion caused by seasons of high and prolonged stress can wound our capacity for joy. Cultivation is a way to protect joy and help prepare the church for a future celebration. We give attention to the soil so that we can reap a full harvest; we cultivate so that we can celebrate.

Cultivate the Soil

The dictionary defines cultivate as "to promote or improve the growth of a plant, crop or other living thing by labor and attention; to produce by culture; to develop or improve by education or training."[7] An environment that values cultivation actively, creatively, and continually invests in the future by paying close attention to the resources and needs at hand.

Cultivation implies that ongoing investment is needed if a harvest of any worth is to follow. Seasons of deep fruitfulness do not happen by accident. Even the most meticulously planned successions can fail if the culture of a church is ill prepared to accept and celebrate the new leader. This is similar to taking a thriving tree that you have spent months and years doting over and then abruptly planting it in parched ground. No matter how healthy the tree is when it is planted, *regardless of the intimate care you've taken during the planting process,* it will not be able to thrive in an environment that is unable to support it.

Undoubtedly, there are many readers who found this book already in a time of crisis or unexpected change. My best counsel to you is to acknowledge that your challenge may necessarily cause you to have to adjust, but most all of the principles still apply to you. If you haven't had the opportunity to be cultivating your soil prior to the actual event, then do what any good landscaper would do: pour on the best fertilizer you can find and watch what happens!

Though it may not look or smell the best, underneath all of that, new life is beginning to sprout. Lamenting what you cannot change does you no good. Embrace where you are and trust God to honor your faith in Him, not the circumstances you've been handed. Create your own timeline using the seven principles and move forward.

As I have noted, the apostle Paul frequently uses the human body as an analogy for how healthy spiritual matters play out (see 1 Corinthians 12). In many ways the succession process parallels that of a medical transplant; for our purposes we'll go with a heart transplant. After the donor has been selected, the body goes through a conditioning process that seeks to prepare the body and take measures to lessen the chance of future organ rejection. It is imperative that this part of the process not be rushed because if the body is not well prepared, it will reject the heart. All of the extensive effort invested to this point will be wasted, often resulting in further—and sometimes fatal—damage to the body. Just as recovering from a failed organ transplant, recovery from a failed succession is no easy task. By the grace of God I know that it is possible to recover and have seen churches rise from the ashes, but if time and effort can be invested in the beginning in order to stave off these chances of infection or host rejection, then hopefully reparative actions can be avoided entirely.

I think it's almost impossible to overstate how challenging this shift can be for the majority of the congregation. I know firsthand of churches that followed the founding pastor with an even more gifted teacher of the Word and visionary leader, only to see that new leader last six months or less in the new environment. In many cases it has absolutely nothing to do with a lack of talent, giftedness, or sense of calling in the new leader. *Rather, it's an underestimation of the process of preparing the staff and congregation to respond and embrace the tunnel of chaos that comes with most every major leadership transition.* Think of any advertisement that is introducing a new medication in to your otherwise healthy body. The list of potential side effects is usually long enough to fill you with fear, causing you to reject what could ultimately help you.

The end goal of succession is the healthy, efficient grafting of a new leader into the environment of an already existing congregation. Successions and organ transplants are not a quick fix. In order for medical transplants—and we would argue this applies to successions as well—to be successful, the body must first be both capable and willing to receive and support a change of this magnitude.

In my extensive reading on this topic and my first hand conversation with dozens of pastors and church leaders; two of the biggest reasons for host rejection in the succession process are (1) the senior pastor is unable, or in some cases unwilling, to step down from his role in a gracious way; and (2) the new senior leader is not embraced by the congregation as God's new leader for the next season of the church's life. In cases where the second is true, it is often the direct result of the first. It will be difficult for any congregation to accept and support the new leader if the former leader is unable/unwilling/unmotivated to prepare them. Because it's all too obvious that these two reasons are where the ice is particularly thin in our crossing, I thought it would be wise to spend some time focusing on specific ways to take preventative measures against these two occurrences. While I realize that the process of cultivation will differ based on the culture of one church to the next, I want to focus on one element of our cultivation process that I believe to be perhaps the single most important change that we embraced at North Way that enabled us to have a nearly *seamless succession* process, especially as it relates to the two above issues.

Involve Multiple Voices

When I began to reflect upon the landscape of failed succession attempts in the church in America, I realized that a vast majority of them happened in contexts where there was one senior pastor who was pretty much the only voice heard by the congregation for multiple years, even decades. Even though the departing senior pastor or leader never intended to have his/her voice as the "one voice that God uses in this church," it is and has been the standard model of the local church in America. Whether a congregation is small or very large, there is usually one prevailing voice that the people come to expect to be inspired of God and worth taking the time to hear each and every week. While in Manhattan several years ago, I witnessed this first hand. Dr. Tim Keller, for whom I have the utmost respect, was, at that time, preaching regularly in a Redeemer Church location that was undisclosed until the time for the message was upon the congregation. When another voice, well qualified and prepared, took the podium to preach, over fifty percent of the worshipers slipped out during the prayer of preparation of the heart! I know things have improved dramatically since then, but this is what happens when people come to expect to hear God through one voice only.

This impacted me enough that I came to realize that I was not doing justice to my church family by being its primary — sometimes only — voice of teaching. As we began to grow into a multi-site congregation, we established a mentoring program for the purpose of training a number of young leaders at North Way. This gave me the opportunity to place quality men in positions of leadership, such as campus pastor, and then provide them with a regular opportunity to teach God's word to the entire congregation, using high-definition video technology. A rotation was established where each campus pastor was given a regular opportunity to preach so that the senior pastor's voice became part of a preaching team of multiple voices rather than the one spiritual leader. Our normal practice is to videotape the Saturday evening message at our largest campus and then use this high-definition quality video at all five locations. We do have about eight weekends a year that are designated as live teaching given at each location by the campus pastor.

The introduction of the teaching team approach did several things. First, it gave an opportunity for younger leaders to develop their communication skills and to learn the discipline of what it takes to prepare a quality message that can be broadly applied across the entire spectrum of those who are part of the North Way Church family. This training required the regular discipline and input of all the members of the teaching team as we would come together to seek God about what needed to be taught to our church family as a whole. This also provided a very objective opportunity for personal feedback and helpful critiques, which then accelerated the ability of each team member to grow in their confidence and capacity as they preached God's word.

Another benefit of this arrangement is that this format brought great validation to each campus pastor and a greater sense of unity to our church as a whole. When one of the other campuses sees their pastor preaching to the entire church, they experience the words of our Church vision statement in flesh: "One church, multiple locations, all generations."

Even beyond the simple concept embodied in our vision statement, the teaching team was integral in our pursuit to cultivate a church culture that would be receptive to upcoming succession changes. This helped prepare the church body to accept something new, and it lessened the chances of host rejection. Because of the rotational teaching format it never became a practice at North Way that "if Pastor Jay was not present, I'm not going to go." *The entire church family began to recognize that they, too, could hear God through different voices in the weekend message.* It provided a measure of protection against our members falling prey to any conscious or unconscious allegiance to the person delivering the Word instead of the Word itself, and lessened the chance of our church rejecting the next leader due to improperly placed loyalties.

From the very beginning I began to sense that the congregation really appreciated and responded to the diversity of style and perspective that was represented across the teaching team. Of course, for others to preach more, that meant I had to preach less. By adopting this model my voice as a senior leader was not usurped in anyway. This model was not based in a relinquishment of position, but in a pursuit to empower the leaders God had placed in my path. For churches that choose to adopt this model it also provides an extra measure of protection from pastoral burnout as there is a routine that allows for a rest from preaching.

The true silver lining in all of this was that when it became time for me to greatly reduce the number of times I would preach in a given year, it was as if nothing out of the ordinary really happened, and it wasn't distressing for the congregation or me. There was no harsh or abrupt transition. In fact, it was quite the opposite. A wonderful measure of continuity was maintained when the new senior leader accepted the position, and the rotation still continued. The members of our congregation had learned to come to each weekend service with the same anticipation and expectation of faith regardless of who was responsible to bring the message that weekend. We have had numerous highly respected leaders visit and even speak at our church. Almost without exception they comment on how powerfully the teaching team acted as a built-in buffer to what is normally a very difficult transition. I had discovered one of the keys of *seamless succession*.

I can report that after more than three years, this strategy is working extremely well. This model helped to unite our multi-site campus model and allowed each pastor's gift of teaching to be used without requiring them to spend twenty to thirty hours each week dedicated to message preparation. It provided an incentive for young men to stay engaged in church ministry because they knew that they have an opportunity to preach the Word; those not gifted in preaching and teaching were invited to serve as campus pastors or other available positions suited to their gifting.

Please hear me when I say that I am not faulting the churches who have embraced, intentionally or not, the one-voice model. There are some extremely gifted preachers and teachers of God's word that I would gladly sit and listen to on a weekly basis. For nearly twenty years I was that person at North Way and came to understand the enormous responsibility and almost impossible demand this can become on anyone who faithfully seeks to teach God's Word. What I realize now, years after implementing a teaching team of multiple voices, is that having only one voice can so easily create a rhythm and culture in the church that makes it very difficult to introduce a successful leadership change.

It may very well be that your church does not have the resources to build a teaching team within the time parameters you have before a necessary succession, or perhaps you're already in the midst of a church succession. If you are in a position where succession may be just a couple of years down the road, it would demonstrate great wisdom to begin to weave at least one other voice into the regular teaching mix so that your congregation begins to understand that the Word of God can come through many different messengers. This is not meant to be an indictment of pastors, but many find it very difficult to imagine themselves as not being that most important voice and can unconsciously undermine their own success by doing so.

When so many people have come to identify a particular voice, and also the heart, of the senior pastor with their own spiritual journey, it can simply be a huge challenge to overcome. Thankfully, in some cases the new leader is received, the new voice is embraced, and the church is able to move ahead in its mission. It is extremely important, however, that we recognize with our eyes wide open that this is the minority and is not what usually happens in even the best of churches. This is where a well-cultivated climate can prove invaluable in preparing both a church and its pastor to thrive both during and after the succession. Initiating this incremental change of adding a teaching team months or even years prior to succession can help pave the way for a smoother deep change when the season of your succession dawns. Now, you, and the church are more likely to glean the positive benefits that can come in this season.

My hope is that by highlighting some steps that can be taken early in the process, it may help avoid a haphazard and reactionary approach to change. You will have space to contemplate as a team, practices that you can implement far in advance. This will lead to cultivating "rich soil" capable of sustaining a healthy succession. Efforts toward cultivation can, and should, take place far before the "initiate" conversation even begins as cultivation helps ready a church for change, regardless of whether this change is centered upon succession or not.

Discussion Questions for Chapter 2: Cultivate

1. On page 34, I make the assertion that "Cultivation is a way to protect joy and help prepare the church for a future celebration." Why is this so?
2. Cultivation is all about preparing for change. Can you think of any place in your church/ministry where you believe that kind of forethought has been introduced?
3. Do you believe that your church/ministry is prepared to hear from the Lord through scriptures and other voices besides the senior pastor/leader? What can you do to help your church to be open to hear from God through other messengers?
4. In my view, establishing the teaching team was perhaps the most important step we took to help cultivate the soil of the heart of the church to receive the seed of God's word through

Is this something that you could begin to do in your church/ministry? If not, what other strategies do you have?

5. On pages 36-37, I assert that even having one other regular voice may help the congregation in a time of transition. Do you think this is the case for you? Why, or why not?

6. I often find that churches are very hesitant to ask for help of any kind, with the exception being for capital stewardship campaigns. If you are a church leader, where would you turn to find help in this most important time in your history?

CHAPTER 3:
COMMUNICATE

Engage Their Trust

I t is of great importance during the "deep change" of succession that communication be given highest priority. The decisions made during this season, and the response (or lack thereof) of the congregation to the future leader will have rippling effects that can lift a church toward greatness or careening to decay. Chances are good that we've all witnessed—at least from a distance—instances of both. I believe that healthy communication is at the very heart of a successful transition. Without it, success will either be unattainable or, at best, short-lived.

The reason for this is that navigating through a deep change requires a delicate balance of emotional and informational communication. If there is a lack of communication with the people whom the change most deeply impacts, something will begin to unravel. Loyalties take time to form. Change is emotional and requires time for new roots to set. In every congregation there will probably be people who need time to grieve change before they are prepared to celebrate change. If the succession is rushed or belittled through a lack of engaging communication, the development of loyalty and trust in the leadership's decision and eventually the new leader may be compromised.

Trust, both in the overall succession process and the incoming leader, is paramount. Although it might not be visible right away, the ramifications of underdeveloped trust later on will be severe. Communication must address the emotions of the change and not only the logistics of the change: "In highly successful change efforts, people find ways to help others see the problems or solutions in ways that influence emotions, not just thought. Feelings then alter behavior sufficiently to overcome all the many barriers to sensible large-scale change. Conversely, in less successful changes, this seeing-feeling-changing pattern is found less often, if at all."[8] This is why the point in our introduction about approaching this season with holy anticipation is so critical. Leadership cannot engage the hope and excitement of the congregation if they are reluctant or despairing of the changes ahead. Remember, people are discerning. If you cannot communicate with authentic confidence, work out your concerns and then share with your people.

The beauty of this is that the 'communicate principle' is fairly simple. If communication is valued as an integral part of the process, and if the congregation is honored and kept well-informed, you will be blessed with a great outcome. Not only are the leadership and transition teams on board, but the entire congregation is championing the new change. The disruption will be minimal, and instead of struggling to convince people of the "right choice" at the end of the process, the Body will be working as a whole to graft in and support the new leader. The succession process can deepen the unity of the entire church.

Invite the Individual

The desired outcome of this very intensive process is, at the end of the day, that the congregation embraces the choice of the transition team and the Elders' Council. By embracing the choice, I mean that they have a sense of confidence in both the process and the integration of the new leader, and they are trusting that the Lord has led those in authority to make the right decision for the good of the whole church. For this kind of outcome to happen, the church cannot feel that the decision was imposed on them. In order to foster corporate ownership and responsiveness in any realm, we must start at the level of the individual. For a succession to work, the individual members that make up the church body must be supportive of the new leader, and this happens by engaging the emotions of the congregation and helping them see and believe that this change is one of wisdom that will benefit the future of the church as a whole. Taking time to help them understand and believe this will fuel the entire succession event.

It is my conviction that in order to foster a well-received succession process at the individual and corporate level the congregation needs to feel *invited* to join the process from the very beginning. What you are asking the church to do in a succession is to accept and graft in something different, other, new. Chances are the congregation is aware that this is more than a decision about a new leader or an isolated personnel event. They know that the new leader means a new season and that things may look different than they used to. Things will change, and those changes will affect them. They may not be quick to articulate it or even be able to articulate it, but many members of the congregation may be concerned that the church they have come to love might drastically change. Consistent, positive, and well-placed communication does a great deal to foster a sense of ownership in the process, and relieve the fear that arises with the realization that things are changing. It leads the congregation to receive the decisions of those who have been delegated the responsibility to make them with a sense of appreciation and support, not skepticism or negativity.

The key to making this change as seamless as possible is to maximize the amount of information you can safely entrust to the congregation *before* these matters are decided. Although we may wish it were different, church members are no different in this regard than any other organization; the absence of information creates a vacuum that is ripe for misinformation and fear. The goal is to communicate content that will minimize fear and uncertainty, remove reasons for resistance, and foster individual and corporate support for the succession, current leader, and future leader.

Even though the members of the congregation are aware of the process, most will not have been involved in the day-to-day details as the members of the transition team and even the Elders' Council will be. Communication is the means by which you allow the congregation to journey alongside you instead of simply announcing the ending to a shocked and surprised audience. People need space to process change. Communication allows them to sense order and be reminded of the grace and leading of God throughout the process. As Mike Myatt aptly states, "Succession needs to be part of the values, vision, strategy, and culture of an organization. . . . It must be viewed as a step forward and not a regression. . . . The truth is succession is a blending of the art and science of leadership, people, positions, philosophies, relationships, culture, and a certainty of execution."[9]

The congregation needs to sense the forward momentum and have their faith bolstered in both the certainty in God's leading and the leadership's capacities to spearhead this change. In order for succession to be successful it cannot be marginalized but must become part of the culture and conversation of its people.

Our desire was to communicate with the congregation on a regular basis about many of the details of the process itself. Even more than that, we wanted to use the platform to allow them to sense our anticipation of and gratitude for the leading of God. We wanted to thank them for journeying alongside us in this change and encourage them to expect positive, exciting, and even more blessed moments in the new season. It also provided time to prepare and grow familiar with the idea of having a new senior leader in place.

We made sure to celebrate the short-term wins as we went along, which helped to sustain the motivation and momentum of our congregation and staff. For example, when the transition team made the decision to focus on our wonderful selection of internal candidates before receiving resumes from those outside of the congregation, we felt that was a positive reassurance worth celebrating. Communicating information like this to the congregation is especially valuable when the succession process may be slow and seemingly quite long. The timeline we had established was, at a minimum, nine to twelve months. It would have been very easy for the work of the transition team to disappear from the corporate radar screen of the church family. We wanted to keep this process at the forefront in their mind and prayers, as it was in ours.

While I realize it is impossible to quantify the difference that these efforts to communicate made in the overall outcome of a succession, I was extremely pleased by the overall affirmation and minimal amount of negative feedback that we received from the church about what was going on. I believe that our church family sensed that their involvement and support was of great importance to this process, and as a result they were more than willing to lend their support.

We always made an effort to communicate important decisions beginning with the highest levels of authority in the church, working our way to the widespread and deeply connected members of our church family. As you might imagine, it would not be a good thing if a member of your Elders' Council, those charged with the final outcome of these processes, heard something from a non-staff church member about a particular step or decision that they had not first heard from the transition team. This type of exchange can be disempowering and may plant seeds of doubt about whether or not they are being valued for the many hours that they have invested in in this very critical decision.

We also understood that to do this well the communication could not solely be top-down. In order to serve our congregation we recognized that communication is a two-way dynamic and we consistently asked the church for feedback on the process or suggestions they might have for better communication. This seemed to go a long way to help everyone embrace, rather than disengage or even resist the process. Church members were encouraged to direct their questions to any church elder who would be sure that they were quickly addressed by the appropriate person on the transition team. By the way, this also prevented some of the "always want to know folks" from over-loading those on the transition team with constant detailed inquiries. I now see that we were able to benefit on a number of levels by providing clear channels of communication rather than an 'open house' approach.

It's worth reaffirming that in a large church, in particular, the challenge of maintaining a sense of approachability by the transition team as well as transparency from the team back to the congregation is no small matter. The key quality that we were seeking to build this process was simply trust. Most experts will often remind you that you cannot trust someone that you don't know, so the only way to build trust is to let yourself be known through regular, transparent, and humble communication.

A Tale of Poor Communication

This seems like an appropriate place to describe in more detail the misstep mentioned in the preface. The entire event took place before the succession process described in these pages was launched. Not quite two years before I knew the succession process should be engaged, we had a staff position come open for a teaching pastor. We brought on to the team a very gifted teacher of the Word with great potential in leadership and casting vision. As the months passed, I could not help but project into the future and see with some extended mentoring and service, that this young man had the raw material from God to possibly become an exceptional senior leader.

However, because the kind of process that I am detailing in this book was not in place, and because North Way had not taken any specific steps to clarify the stream of communication, it wasn't long before the possibility of this individual becoming a candidate had to be taken off the table. What moved this event from simply disappointing to somewhat damaging was the absence of a clear communication process, which allowed many inaccurate stories to begin to undermine the entire experience. Please keep in mind that I am shrinking about nine months of experience into a few sentences, but this difficult lesson was learned at a significantly high price within our church as well as for the young man and his family. I know, first hand, how quickly something positive can become a negative in this matter of succession, and this event made it painfully obvious to us that we needed a much more structured and highly interactive communication plan to allow us to undergo a future positive and lasting succession experience.

It's very likely that some who are reading this book have been through a negative experience when it comes to succession or transition. The statistics would bear out such a conclusion. Through my experience I discerned a few axioms that proved helpful in our journey toward healing and redeeming the trust of those impacted. First, those who were involved or responsible for the unsuccessful attempt should be given much grace. As I have learned, theirs is not an easy assignment.

Second, transparency with the full congregation and an honest evaluation of why things did not work out should be forthcoming very quickly after the event. The longer the gap between the failed succession and statement of disclosure, the more likely it is for people to speculate and even create false explanations that then must be corrected. And the more time passes, the easier it is to forget specific things that need addressing in order for the failure not to repeat itself.

Third, I have found that most sincere church members are very forgiving of those who humbly accept responsibility and are readily open to a time of restoration and starting over. I would recommend that at least a couple of new people be introduced to the transition team to add perspective and perhaps bring fresh energy to starting the process.

In another small group in which I participate, we had hit a wall of spiritual progress. We all knew it, prayed about it, changed materials we were studying, and so on. But when we added not one, but two new couples, it was transformed literally overnight! New input, new perspectives, and the anticipation of something different taking place breathed fresh life in to our group.

To recap, when a negative succession event occurs:

1. Give grace to all involved (Eph.5:32).
2. If the word has spread, have an opportunity for the entire church to hear your explanation.
3. Humbly ask forgiveness and appeal for a time of healing, restoration, and new perspectives (Col.3:13).

Logistics of Communication

The logistics of communication will vary based on the size and style of the church, but I thought it might be beneficial to provide a brief overview of our communication plan. Throughout the entire process bimonthly update emails were sent out to all members (regular mail to those had not given us an electronic address). We nominated one person from the transition team to be responsible for maintaining an open line of communication with the church family. As I mentioned previously, we wanted the communication to be a constant reminder to the congregation of the wonderful changes stirring. We were blessed to have a staff member who had experience in both HR and PR who was willing to take the point position for communication. We felt that having one person be the public voice of the succession process would ensure that information unfolded with continuity. We protected this person by making sure that people brought their questions through someone else's authority so that she could not be overwhelmed without some kind of prescreening, though this turned out to never become a problem.

In addition, every month or so, a different member of the transition team would address the entire congregation and give a verbal report of the current status of the process, making sure to communicate the deep appreciation we had for the support that we felt from the church family.

As the outgoing senior pastor, I felt it was my responsibility to communicate the process and progress of the transition team and the ultimate decision that they made to those who were involved in positions of leadership/staff within the church. This posture led to several direct benefits such as:

- It served to reassure every member of our church staff that they were getting reliable and fact-based information enabling them to confidently address concerns or questions that arose from the congregation.
- It provided me an opportunity to effectively communicate my personal support of the process and the final decision to those who were most affected by the change of leadership, thus reducing the possibility of uncertainty within the staff population.

Now, a word about communicating with outside media, or if you prefer, the secular press. We believed that it was in the best interest of our church to let the public media know our church was purposefully and expectantly moving into a season of change even before an actual date had been set. We sent a press release at the outset of the succession process and another one once we had announced our decision to the congregation. This kind of proactive outreach with the secular media actually proved to be a great blessing to our church as many were able to witness the unity of our church by observing how we celebrated the departing pastor and welcomed the succeeding pastor. As a brief side note, we had literally scores of people outside of our church family who commented on the orderly and positive way that our transition took place. Most everyone, especially people in business, knows how difficult a transition of this magnitude can be.

Establishing New Relationships

Not long after the new lead pastor, Pastor Scott, had taken his role of leadership, my wife, Carol, and I made an investment in reaching out to those who are the committed, faithful and invested members of our church. These are people who are not necessarily in titled positions of authority within the church, who provide great support to the continuing mission and vision of the church through either significant financial donations or through positions of relational leadership.

It is essential for the new pastoral leader to be engaged and supported by those with the monetary capacity and natural leadership that have been integral in helping the church thrive and be fruitful. Whoever first stated the following axiom is not clear to me, but nonetheless, I believe it to be absolutely true: you very likely will not support someone you don't trust. And, it's nearly impossible to trust someone that you don't know. Therefore, Carol and I made it a priority to introduce Pastor Scott and his wife, Tina, to about one hundred people that we invited to our home over several nights. These gatherings were informal, relatively brief and included a great deal of interaction amongst the people who were invited.

It may seem like a small and insignificant detail, but the fact that we held these get-togethers in our home rather than on the church property seem to add an extra measure of support, affection, and trust. I also believe that affirming the new senior pastor as *my pastor* went a long way to validate his call. We all know that it simply takes time to build a level of personal trust and confidence in any individual, but the unconditional affirmation that my endorsement of the decision provided would likely help a number of people to make that journey to trust much more quickly, thus allowing Scott to transition into his role with greater levels of confidence and support. The sense of corporate enthusiasm and anticipation by such a significant number of devoted leaders in our church ministry remains a moment that I will not ever forget. Simply measured by response, ninety-six percent of all the people invited to the two-hour event that occurred in the middle of the week on a few occasions, was a powerful statement of the desire people had to really get to know and affirm their new senior pastor.

Regardless of the details of your church's succession event, make it a priority from the beginning to communicate regularly, transparently and passionately, throughout the process. Invite the congregation to walk alongside you and support this new season that God is ushering in. Be sure to give focused attention to those who have invested a great deal of time, effort, and resources under the former leadership as they will often be the core group of people championing the new leader. Gratitude should be in abundant supply as you bring closure to this step of the process.

This is, by most accounts, one of the biggest decisions your Church has ever made. When the Lord had "good news," He didn't hesitate to "let the whole world know" by bright stars and angelic beings. Since neither of these were readily available, a nicely placed press release and of course a salvo of tweets and hashtags seemed to get the job done, though with admittedly less awe than the arrival of the Savior. (All angelic choirs were booked that week-end.)

Discussion Questions for Chapter 3: Communicate

1. On page 42, I affirm that trust in both the person and the process is critically important in the succession plan. Do you agree? Why, why not?
2. This is a chapter on communication. However, I make the point that such communication must be emotional as well as informational. Why is that so?
3. What will normally happen when the church does not receive communication from those in authority on any issue? How does misinformation affect the church going forward?
4. Clear, consistent, and authentic communication invites all the people in the process of change. Describe how that should make your church/ministry embrace the final outcome.

5. On the other side of the coin, how would you propose to receive communication from the church/ministry in a personal and sensitive manner?
6. If your church leadership does experience a setback, what is the best course of action going forward? (p. 48)
7. On page 50, I talk about hosting an event with key leaders in my home in order to personally introduce our incoming senior leader to those who may not know him well. Why is something like this so important, and what kind of message does it send to the leaders?

CHAPTER 4:
INVESTIGATE

Assess the Need

The "Investigate" phase involves a diligent and disciplined process of identifying and discussing the needs of the congregation and then determining how these needs inform the decisions surrounding the succession. The qualities of the person that will be the next senior leader should in some identifiable ways fit closely with both the current and anticipated needs of the congregation.

Assessing the church's needs should come *prior* to the search for suitable candidates and/or any assessment of the strengths and weaknesses of any potential in-house candidates. The whole investigation process can be shortchanged if the needs of the church are not taken into account prior to the search. It's far easier to figure out what you're looking for *before* you begin your journey and thereby bypass a great deal of confusion, time, and heartache.

Assessing church needs is an assignment that extends outside the mission of the transition team alone; it should include the input of the ruling body of that local church. For us, a great deal of discussion took place with the leaders of many ministries in the church to help to discern what they felt was important as we moved into the next season of ministry together. Thankfully, with the wide diversity of the transition team and the input of a number of volunteer ministry leaders, we were able to clearly identify the specific strengths that we were seeking in our future leader.

The end goal is to find a leader that will thrive within an already existing congregation and be able to effectively serve and lead them.

In order to search for the best candidate you must first identify the already existing church culture, acknowledging its weaknesses and strengths, that they must be able to support and lead. In some cases the leader will have a weakness that parallels a weakness within the church. At this point you will be able to determine if they are capable and willing to delegate this area, or if this could prove problematic for the future growth of both the potential leader and the church. This process will also help identify areas where they may need additional support in the adjustment period. These things can only be addressed based on the amount of information and understanding that you have during the search process. Let's be very clear to state that *denial is not an option* in this assessment.

It's probably fair to say that most of the men and women with whom I served at North Way would acknowledge that one of my strengths is the ability to cast vision. No matter what the environment in which I was placed, it wasn't long before I was asking myself the question, "what does a better future look like in this particular ministry?" I considered it part of my role as senior pastor to inspire and encourage my leaders to ask that same question. Under my leadership the church has grown with a natural bent towards vision. As a result, we have a wonderful abundance of vision in a number of areas of ministry. The flipside of this strength, however, is that it's easy to develop a natural deficiency in following through with these initiatives. When I was leading well, I would always be sure that an appropriate staff member was willing and able to own the process of finishing what I had successfully launched. It takes a gifted person to fully implement the vision of someone else. There were organizational weaknesses within the church that tended to parallel my own personal weaknesses. When we began to assess the church for weaknesses, we noticed that there were several areas in our ministry and staff that could greatly benefit from someone with a high capacity for administration and management, able to address some of the weaknesses in the church that arose during my years as senior pastor.

Please note that I am in no way suggesting that the succeeding pastor should be the exact opposite of the current pastor. In some cases this could prove disastrous. What I am suggesting is that the task of assessing the needs of the church should clarify, narrow, and inform the search focus. This identified need in our church for administrative follow-through became a core strength the transition team looked for in a potential future senior leader. Vision was still an important quality to us, but we also recognized the necessity and benefit of hiring someone who had a desire to develop clear support strategies and help implement already-existing visions.

Many churches are just seeking to find a younger and fresher version of the person they have had in leadership for the previous twenty or more years. As you begin to listen to God's voice through the needs of your congregation, be open to His leading—even if it takes you in a direction you weren't expecting.

Draft a Description

Assessing the needs of the church is the first step. From the content gained as a result, the transition team is then able to draft something akin to a position description or more simply, a job description. Having a specific, stated, prayed-for, and agreed-upon description helps to clarify the giftedness of the leader needed in the next season. I also found that it helps foster a sense of agreement and unity among the leadership and the transition/search teams throughout the process. The description should be reviewed often throughout the search process as it will serve to protect the integrity of the search. It becomes less likely for candidates to be selected based on personality preferences or previous relationships when a clear candidate description has been prayerfully and unanimously agreed upon.

This is an enormously *important point*, and I want to do justice to what implications it has on the succession process. It's fair and accurate to say that most churches and other organizations don't take the necessary time to do this assessment well, if at all. In fact, I can name three relatively healthy, stable growing congregations where the senior pastor simply announced his departure would be coming in the next three to six or twelve months. In all cases, he recommended that a specific in-house candidate be appointed to the position. There was no assessment of the current needs and direction of the church, no draft of a position description. It doesn't take a degree in psychology to see what an awkward position this creates for everyone.

If the executive pastor (an in-house candidate) is endorsed by the senior pastor but not chosen by the transition or succession team, he's deeply hurt, and the congregation is usually greatly affected. If the executive pastor is appointed to the position and in the next months or even year or two he fails to lead the church well, then the hurt and division can be even more painful. It is imperative that everyone involved understands the depth of relational loyalty and even biblical affection that gets built in these long-term, in-house relationships.

If circumstances begin to reveal that it is not a good fit, there is simply no easy way to gracefully end the relationship apart from an unusual level of maturity on the part of the executive pastor. It is infinitely better to embrace the investigative process now and know the suitability of the candidate before he or she takes the position.

Once the hard work of drafting a position description had been undertaken, our transition team was then ready to investigate the possibility that the very person that they were looking for was already part of our current team of leaders. Selecting a candidate who is already known by the church and comfortable with the culture is clearly preferable as it drastically reduces the amount of change and adjustment needed for both parties.

We have all heard stories of excellent leaders who excelled in one church culture and yet were not able to make the change to embrace a different culture, even though it may have appeared to be very similar. Too often a new pastor relocates to the area, gets his family settled into a new school and all the rest, and then six months or so into the process realizes that it just isn't going to work. It saddens me that it seems that some form of this story takes place every single day in a church here in America. Because of these extremely difficult and oftentimes painful situations, it is in the best interest of the church family that initial consideration for the future successor is given to those who are currently serving on the pastoral or leadership team.

We were blessed to have four excellent teaching pastors who deserved consideration for the role of senior or lead pastor of our church. I'm very aware that this is a highly unusual situation for most churches, but I want to share some of the details of that process so that you might consider how you would evaluate one or multiple in-house candidates.

Interviewing In-house

Based on my research and conversation with other people in the field of succession, the most common mistake that occurs when hiring in-house is to either overlook the potential weaknesses of a candidate or overrate their abilities due to a previously established bond of friendship. The frank reality is that it can be extremely difficult to lay down some of those closely held personal feelings for the sake of truly objective evaluation. The goal of a succession process is not to pick the leader that you get along with the best, but the leader who will be the best fit to serve the needs of the congregation moving forward. This is why it is so critical to identify need-based criteria to help protect the integrity and unity of the search.

Each of our in-house candidates was asked to fill out a rather exhaustive questionnaire, including everything from theological questions, personal background, and experiences, to a self-analysis of perceived strengths and limitations. (Some illustrations of these questions are available at my website: www.passavantleadership-group.com.)

We gave the candidates a substantial amount of time to thoughtfully and prayerfully fill out the questionnaire because we felt it was important for us to understand each individuals understanding of their desire, sense of capacity, and conviction with regard to fulfilling this final position. We didn't want their answers pressured by a hurried timeline. The results of the hard work that these men invested in the initial questionnaires were invaluable—to them, to us, to our ministry with them going forward. As none of these candidates had ever applied for a senior pastor role in any other location, we had the privilege of engaging them in a bit of self-discovery as well as the possibility of being the right choice to lead our church family into the future.

Every member of the transition team personally reviewed the questionnaires of each candidate. We wanted to give appropriate time to every candidate's responses and do justice to the hard work they had invested in writing their thoughts and convictions. We scheduled several meetings for the purpose of evaluating their responses and discussing and making notes about things that we learned concerning each candidate in terms of their suitability, strengths, weaknesses, and to some degree, their sense of calling.

In addition to undergoing our own process of interviewing the in-house candidates, we also chose to invest in a custom designed executive skills assessment, which was quite an undertaking. As this was our first experience with succession, we felt it was wise to engage an executive firm that was more experienced in the process of skills assessment and personal evaluation. Through a close personal connection, we were able to partner with one of the nation's premier companies to participate in this portion of the process with us. Their headquarters is in our city, making the interaction with them and our entire team a clear and cost effective decision.

The company we engaged has been in the field of executive training and assessment for three decades. As a result, they had access to much more technically advanced processes and emerging technologies that enabled us to understand in significant detail the strengths and weaknesses of each candidate. Beyond that, they approached each candidate with a completely neutral and objective point of view. The company was able to conduct their evaluations without any preconceived impressions formed of the leaders, which helped maintain the overall integrity of the search and protect us from decisions based on personal preference or pre-established relationships.

Along with extensive personal interviews, there were a few simulations that each candidate had to encounter. It was pretty challenging for everyone involved. Following the interviews a highly experienced analyst drew up a detailed personal report for each candidate. As you might imagine, this fairly exhaustive process resulted in evaluations that gave us very valuable information on how each candidate might respond to certain situations and also how they would best be encouraged and supported in whatever role of ministry they were called to pursue. Keep in mind that most of the material in this part of the process had to do with leadership skills and overall character development, which was insightful for both the candidates and the church as we moved forward in ministry.

I am aware that bringing in an outside agency can be viewed as nonessential, but I believed then, and even more so now in retrospect, that these interviews provided helpful information on each candidate and also gave them insight into how they would best work going into the future. *It is in no way a substitute for the primary qualifications of spiritual leadership. It is, however, a very helpful balance to that spiritual equation.* I would even make a case that testing of this sort would be of significant importance in any ministry setting that wanted to bring out the best in its leadership team. Even if none of the candidates were selected for the senior pastor role, this process proved to be a rich investment into the men as leaders and into our ministry culture. The candidates felt valued, heard, and understood; and it affirmed to the entire congregation how seriously we were taking this decision.

I recognize that not everyone might be willing to spend the resources that it takes to do such testing, but whether you engage a very professional, high-caliber corporation or simply an experienced consultant who has a toolkit of resources, there's no question that outside evaluation at this important crossroads is a valuable resource. If your desire is to maintain long-term relationships with an individual even if they do not step into the role as senior leader, this can still provide the kind of quality training they need to maximize their potential. This information was valuable whether or not the candidate was chosen to fill the lead role.

An interesting dynamic that took place during the several weeks of the investigate phase was the interaction between the four candidates. Each of these men knew that the process required confidentiality and there was not to be any conversation around the specifics of the various interviews and testing. Although this may sound like a reasonable request, every one of the candidates commented on how difficult it was to maintain natural day-to-day relationships while going through such arduous and disciplined testing.

In fact, we later discovered that two of the four candidates had wrestled with the possibility of dropping out of the process simply because of the overall weight of the demands on their already full schedules.

However, it was not only the time burden, it was the awareness that the candidates had of one another and the likelihood (in their own mind) that their chances of being selected at this time in their spiritual journey was not very positive.

In retrospect, my admiration for all the candidates who endured this process we were designing as we went along should have been more clearly expressed on a more frequent basis.

The best part of the outcome was not just that we found a very capable and committed person within the group of four, but that all the men continued on in their service to their respective campuses after learning that they had not been selected. In my view, this was an exemplary demonstration of humility and self-sacrifice.

Broadening to External Candidates

Now that you have a pretty clear sense of the thoroughness with which we evaluated our in-house candidates, it's probably time to address the question that was on all of our minds. What would we do if none of the four in-house candidates seem to be an appropriate fit for the position? Make no mistake, we knew there would be huge implications if that was the case. This matter had been discussed by the transition team and the Elders' Council during the early stages of our meetings. We came to the preliminary conclusion that if an in-house candidate was not available, that two specific things would result: (1) we would engage a high-integrity, well-respected search firm to help us identify potential external candidates based on the extensive preparation that we had done over the previous months. In fact, we felt that we would be much better prepared to deal with a search firm because of the investment in time and relationships that we had already made. (2) I would continue in the role of senior pastor for an additional period of time rather than create some sort of unpredictable interim situation, which really doesn't do much to reassure the congregation and adds an additional measure of change into an already difficult season.

If the outcome of the in-house search had not provided a viable candidate, the first step for the transition team would have been to make a list of our personal contacts from other ministries anywhere in the country. A personal recommendation from a trusted friend who knows and understands your organizational DNA is a way to discover potential candidates who may not even be looking. We all know of situations where someone who seems to be content where they are, had no idea of an even better position that would maximize their Kingdom fruitfulness. Start there.

Next, the Internet provides an opportunity to do a limited amount of informal searching through numerous sites that are available at little or no cost. If no one is easily identified through personal connections or Internet sites, then move to the next serious step in your process by engaging a quality search or staffing firm. In today's world, there are a number of effective firms that have already done a good deal of groundwork on behalf of their client who is looking for a change. In my opinion, it's a worthwhile investment.

All of this takes time, so we knew that some strategy needed to be in place for those who had already given many months to search. The Elders' Council, transition team, and I were in agreement that if it was necessary to extend our search to include external candidates, everyone would have the opportunity to take some time to reevaluate their commitment to the process in order to determine whether or not they could continue on.

You can be sure that all of us were praying that one of the four candidates from our in-house team would be the man that God had in mind. Though we greatly valued one another's commitment to the process and enjoyed much of what we were doing as a Kingdom investment, we all recognized that it was a process that was too demanding to carry on indefinitely. Thankfully, after considerable heartfelt dialogue and extensive interviewing, we knew that we had the man that God had chosen for us. It's worth noting that when we didn't agree about a particular candidate at first, the commitment to openly discuss the concern almost always led to resolution. *Don't underestimate the grace that is released when a team is willing to share openly about their concerns or convictions.*

It's hard to do justice to the positive shift within the transition team when we knew with certainty that the candidate God had been directing to us was someone that we already knew well and all that remained was to prepare the candidate and the congregation for this most important season of transition. We were still pretty far from the finish line, but the critical decision had been made!

Discussion Questions for Chapter 4: Investigate

1. Why is it so valuable to have an accurate assessment of the needs in the church before searching for a candidate? Very few churches seem to take this vitally important step of assessment before the search. Why? (p. 53-54)

2. In many cases that I studied, the church seemed to select a younger person with the same gift mix as the outgoing pastor. Why is this not necessarily a good idea?

3. How does a clear job description serve to greatly facilitate this decision? What heartache does it enable you to avoid?

4. What are some of the benefits of being able to find a candidate who is already on your team? (p. 56)

5. Why is the addition of a totally objective evaluation such a worthwhile investment in this decision? What prevents your leadership from doing that in one way or another?

6. On pages 60-61, I address the possibility of having to go elsewhere to find a suitable candidate for this position. What are the drawbacks to this approach? What are the benefits?

7. If you find that you need help in identifying a candidate, where would you turn?

CHAPTER 5:
INTEGRATE

I n late April of 2011, the transition team made their unanimous
recommendation to the Elders' Council to extend the position to
Pastor Scott. Scott prayed about it with his wife and closest mentors and accepted the call. The Elders' Council agreed that a brief
announcement should be made to the congregation communicating
our joy and excitement, peace and unity, in the unanimous decision
of inviting Pastor Scott to accept the position of senior pastor. The
public transition would not occur until September 30, 2011, nearly a
five-month runway where I (Jay) would remain in my position and
focus my best energies in helping Scott, the staff, and congregation
prepare for the official transition.

Though five months was probably more time than necessary, it
did allow us to communicate extensively, celebrate appropriately
(more on this in the following chapter), and seek to address any
potential issues that could have proven problematic if this stage had
been rushed. For example, Pastor Scott did not have a replacement
in mind for his position as executive pastor. Following weeks of dialogue, we agreed to move ahead with a very focused executive team
including several of our pastors and a couple of folks who had significant hands-on involvement in managing the ministry and entered
what we will now refer to as the "integrate" phase.

The integrate phase exists in this small window of time beginning when the new leader is announced and ending at the date of the
official transfer of leadership/authority. During these months, the current leader and leadership team have a vitally important role to play.
At this point in the succession the current senior leader is still in the

position of operational and spiritual authority, and because of this the staff and leadership will—intentionally or unintentionally—watch the relationship between the current and future leader for direction on how to navigate these changes. When the current pastor is able to view this departing season of senior leadership not as a loss of value or opportunity to disengage and go on an extended vacation, but as a chance to intentionally integrate the new leader into the fabric of the church, the whole feel of the church can change.

Although it may seem difficult to believe, it's during these very important weeks where many churches drop the ball. The big decision has been made, but now the important steps of integration are overlooked, which may lead to a feeling of lack of appreciation or perhaps a perceived devaluing of an important core leader or ministry. It's my conviction that the responsibility to facilitate these face-to-face interactions and personal connections is the direct responsibility of the outgoing senior leader. If he (or she) requests the help of other key elders, that increases the possibility of a truly seamless transition.

The suggested approach of a gradual integration prior to the big day involves a great deal of intentional support and interaction with the new leader—especially on the part of the current leader. In this approach the candidate does not sit on the sidelines waiting but is invited to come observe and participate in the daily undertakings of the church. This stage has the potential to be truly energizing, strategic, and revealing. It is an opportunity for the new leader to be introduced to key leaders and staff, allowing the outgoing senior leader time to facilitate the relationships and connections that are most critical to the effective launch of a new leadership figure. In many ways, what happens during the integrate phase will have more to do with our goal of a *seamless succession* than almost anything else. The church cannot help but be motivated by such active participation between the two leaders. A well-executed integration phase creates a sense of positive momentum that will carry the new leader through the first months after the official transition.

One of the reasons I believe this method to be most effective is because it allows the future leader to focus on learning the culture, programs, staff, and people without the added strain of full responsibility. He has a chance to grow familiar with the needs, ideas, and concerns of those whom this decision will most impact. The relational and administrative learning curve lessens so that when the big day does come, the leader is stepping into a familiar environment, automatically minimizing fear, and more importantly, reducing avenues of possible failure.

In the "Cultivate" chapter, I discussed in depth how to help prepare the congregation to accept and celebrate the upcoming changes involved in succession. As I shift to this next season of integration, the content of communication will narrow in focus. Instead of cultivating the congregation to prepare for broad changes, you will begin to prepare the church, leadership and staff to welcome a *specific* new leader. The focus of this stage is on slowly, carefully integrating the selected candidate into day-to-day operations and establishing an authority exchange that paves the way for a seamless hand off.

Certain aspects of the integrate phase may change depending on whether you're transitioning to an in-house or external candidate. Let's look at both scenarios.

Integrating an In-house Candidate

As I have mentioned before, the selection of an in-house candidate makes a seamless integration process that much more attainable. The strategy here involves a deliberate spirit of confidence and expressed enthusiasm at every level. The in-house candidate already knows the church culture intimately and therefore the brunt of integration will deal with operational and relational details most relevant to the upcoming position. The goal is to help flatten the learning curve by identifying strategic areas to slowly integrate the new leader even prior to his official acceptance of the position. Time and energy should be spent initially identifying these areas of ministry and relationships that are critical to the ongoing health and productivity of the church as these will be where a significant amount of energies and resources during the integrate stage should be directed. For North Way specifically, one of the most central areas where we had determined to focus our integration efforts, especially if the leader chosen was an external candidate, was on was the teaching team because of its very critical relationship to our undergirding ministry strategy. We felt that it would be very helpful for the incoming pastor to be able to hear the heart of the other teaching pastors and listen to their messages for a few months before stepping into the rotation. It's worth noting that the person chosen for the position had not been part of the teaching team prior to this decision.

I'll discuss two examples of how North Way approached this method of gradual integration, and while the areas of ministries may differ in detail, the overall approach can apply to almost any situation.

First, we had a specific commitment as a church staff to meet on a weekly basis for approximately one hour every Wednesday for purposes of both inspiration and communication. The common practice was for the senior pastor to lead the devotional content and the executive pastor would lead the strategic and operational part of the meeting.

As you might imagine, very little had to change about this important gathering as Pastor Scott had responsibility for the implementation of our strategies and details of our vision. However, it seemed like a very good interim step to give Pastor Scott the opportunity to bring the devotional thoughts leading up to the transition weekend so that he could be celebrated in that new role. I also used that platform to openly, enthusiastically, and frequently affirm Pastor Scott's calling and giftedness in the new role of senior leader. And certainly, there were weeks when I would ask for Scott to provide the devotional leadership simply to begin to build the trust, appreciation, and support that he needed from the staff as their spiritual leader. There's no perfect way to measure how this positively influenced the overall transition, but by an objective evaluation, this seemed to allow the staff to fully embrace Pastor Scott and yet still show appreciation for my increasingly limited role.

With the elders and staff in particular, my priorities with Pastor Scott were to inform and affirm. Candidly, I don't think it would be possible to overstate how important both of those qualities were needed by everyone involved. Inform and affirm! This was a great investment in terms of making a *seamless succession*, as a great deal of integration will center around relational issues such as the development and deepening of trust both in the position and person of the new leader. I made it a priority to affirm Pastor Scott at every opportunity with the elders, staff and church volunteer leaders, small group leaders, and even weekend service attendees. It's important to recognize just how much the people of the church are reading how both leaders are handling the decision and what that means for the future of the church. We didn't want to leave any room for doubt or second-guessing the decision. We believed that the Spirit of God had led us to the decision through the detailed process I have described, and we had every confidence in His favor as we progressed, and it was a joy to readily communicate this to all involved.

I noticed that Scott would occasionally use his influence from the platform to reference my new role and perhaps contributions to getting us where we were, and I had many opportunities to do the same for him. In a way that I don't fully understand, it was also somewhat reassuring for some of the staff to know that we (Carol and I) were still around and that we had nothing but commitment and like-minded resolve to advance the kingdom even when the church was no longer under our leadership and direction.

Behind the scenes, Pastor Scott and I met at least once weekly to discuss the ministries in which I had had a more intimate level of involvement than he previously enjoyed, so that he would feel better equipped to take on those new opportunities and responsibilities when the official transition took place. What made that time so valuable was that we were both in new territory. Our faith was being tested in different ways but dramatically enough that we could identify with each other. I'll cover this more in depth in the "Evaluate" section.

Second, another area where I felt it important to give Scott more of a hands-on experience was in our weekly elders' prayer meeting. Our elders are committed to prayer and many of them will come on Saturday mornings from 8 to 9 AM specifically to intercede on behalf of the church and its many members and ministries. I would often provide leadership for that prayer meeting by selecting scriptures, identifying the focus and needs, and so on. During this interim season I turned that responsibility over to Pastor Scott. I knew that Scott understood the kind of leadership needed for sustained prayer involvement.

It's interesting to note that not long after the transition took place, Scott made a very wise decision in engaging the most devoted and mature elders to provide leadership in facilitating the Saturday morning prayer time. Even though he would still participate, he did not have to do the preparation and communication required for this time to be worthwhile. It was a strong and wise move.

One final comment on the dynamics involved with the selection of an in-house leader. It is important that everyone recognizes that responsibility for leadership yet remains with the outgoing senior leader until the day of official transition arrives. There needs to be clarity in this because the church's mission and vision requires leadership even in the midst of succession, and it can hurt momentum when staff or church members do not know who to report to or follow. Though the senior pastor's role is about to change, during those final months, it is imperative that the senior pastor champion the process of integration with wholehearted focus and authority. This will expedite the trust and security of all others involved in every area of ministry.

Integrating an External Candidate

The transition team knew that though selecting a candidate who was already part of the team was highly preferred, it is not always the right choice. In fact, I want to reiterate that although we did select our executive pastor to become the new senior leader, that selection is not normally one that works well. Needless to say, the level of disappointment and pain that is often caused by these forced internal succession attempts can be very damaging. Make no mistake; these kinds of situations can not only slow a church's momentum, they can literally bring them to separation and loss.

In our situation, we recognized from the beginning that we needed to be open to the idea that we may not have the right person for our future from within and be prepared to look outside as well. An aversion to this can limit and blind the focus of the transition team. Although I recognize that I cannot offer the same detailed encouragement in this scenario as we did not personally undergo this part of the search, we did give a great deal of forethought to this possibility and had a detailed plan in mind. I want to spend a bit of time discussing the intended plan as I know a large number of succession plans end up including a search for external candidates.

First, the members of the transition team would reevaluate and hopefully be able to recommit themselves to be available for the next season of the search, which could require an additional year of time and energy. It was not a given that everyone could remain involved because of the heavy demand required to do the initial in-house search, and if we needed to include additional transition team members, we were ready to reassemble a team prepared to dedicate themselves fully to this mission.

Following this, the team would have reconvened to review the previous candidate description. There may be a few additional items that require discussion now that the search has broadened outside the scope of the church family, such as whether there would be opportunities for accompanying staff members to be selected by the candidate. As with the investigate stage, any non-negotiable need should be agreed upon prior to the search.

I had agreed to continue in the role for one more year if we reached a point where the search needed to extend to include external candidates for consideration. The congregation would be informed if or when the search made this decision as we would want them to know that their prayerful support was profoundly appreciated and still very much needed. If the pastor is able to make a commitment to extending his position in these circumstances, it can provide a wonderful measure of additional confidence in the process. The transition and elder teams will not feel rushed to make a hasty decision or shortchange the process by choosing an internal candidate when it would be wise to consider other options that may be better suited to the church needs and community.

We had already contacted a highly respected national search firm and were prepared to engage them as soon as the decision was made. We were assured that they would help us find suitable candidates within a very narrow timeframe. We had been down the same road a couple of times for other positions that we could not fill internally. On our side we would have engaged in the same process of candidate investigation and evaluation as described in the earlier chapter.

Once a viable and unanimously agreed-upon candidate was found, the plan was to bring him on board as soon as possible. It would then become the primary responsibility of the senior pastor and executive pastor to help the new leader integrate with the elders, staff, and ultimately the entire congregation, in that order.

Models of Integration

There are many different models and strategies that one can consider when it comes to integrating a new (whether internal or external) leader with the elders, staff, key ministry volunteers, and the church family. In our culture, I believe that there should be some sort of highly relational plan where the current senior pastor and executive pastor take the lead on helping integrate the new pastor into the various roles and relationships related to his new position. I know of other churches that use the shadow method where the new leader simply walks with the senior pastor through all of his duties and learns as he goes. In some cases the incoming senior leader attended nearly every meeting for four to eight weeks, taking copious notes and learning to put names and faces together, all in an effort to make the transition as seamless as possible.

I've made a few references to of the ongoing life of the church during the succession process, but I want to hone in on this for a little bit. It may seem to those on the transition team and even some of the staff that your best energies are going into this succession process, especially if the in-house pastors are the ones that are dealing with the process. If intentional forethought is not given to what is needed to provide visionary leadership during this undertaking and the season of adjustment after the naming, the church may begin to stall at the very time that you want and need the church to be growing in anticipation, mission, and passion for Christ.

Another benefit of this gradual integration is that it is easier to keep the staff engaged and involved. At this point it's very natural for staff to feel caught between the tension of hopeful anticipation and cautious apprehension about how this change in leadership will affect their daily work. With the new leader selected and the big day approaching, the current leader can feel disconnected or even displaced. Roles can become confused, loyalties blurred, and decisions can be put on hold until the new leader steps up. The effects of this can be devastating, resulting in the new leader walking into a team that feels undervalued, exhausted, and confused.

Obviously, there are no firm parameters for this kind of integration process, but I feel that it would be about three months and would ideally happen in a slower season of ministry. If such an arrangement can be made, it simply allows some time for the new pastor to breathe the air of the new church culture that he has been called to lead. When his time for teaching and leadership does arrive, he will have a fairly long runway to know and understand the culture, needs, and strengths.

There was enthusiastic engagement of Scott as the new leader, and yet I continued to feel valued and welcomed by the staff and church family in my new role throughout this new season. The season of celebration had finally arrived!

Discussion Questions for Chapter 5: Integrate

1. The integrate phase often determines whether the new leader will start with momentum or a strong headwind. Why is this so important to manage well?
2. Why is gradual integration the most preferred way to make the transition? (p. 64)
3. In this chapter I introduce the idea of understanding the church culture. What are some of the defining characteristics of your church culture as you understand them?
4. What are some of the most important things that need to happen with the incoming senior pastor/leader during this integration phase? Likewise, what are some things that the outgoing senior pastor/leader might do to help facilitate this transition?
5. This is also a delicate time when the congregation is anticipating the new leader but watching the outgoing leader for his/her response. Why is the commitment to "inform and affirm" so important in this phase?

6. In our particular circumstance, we made a commitment to meet every week in order to keep everything as transparent and positive as possible. What would you do if such a meeting with the outgoing and incoming leader is not possible?

7. Though we did not need to take the step of looking for an external candidate, we were fully prepared to do so and had already made the critical connections. Where would you turn if you need help in finding an external candidate in a timely manner?

CHAPTER 6:
CELEBRATE

"Then I will thank you in front of the great assembly.
I will praise you before all the people." Psalm 35:18

"Sing to the LORD, for he has done glorious things;
let this be known to all the world." Isaiah 12:5

Continue the Genesis Rhythm

In the midst of a beautiful flurry of creation activity, of seas receding and mountains pressing up from dry earth, the tone shifts. After six stunning days of world-making activity, everything stops: "He rested from all the work of creating that He had done" (Gen 2:3). He rested, enjoyed, marveled at the works of His hands, and then commanded us to do the same. He carved out space to foster contemplation and gratitude—and celebration. He carved out space to stop working and breathe deeply, to respond; to "[b]e still and know that I am God" (Ps 46:10). There's a tendency in our culture to skip over this part, both in our individual lives and as a corporate body. We want to keep right on going, right on creating. We're used to the adrenaline of the creating part. Perhaps we think our work too important to stop; rest feels too unproductive. Or our guess is that most simply don't realize the deeper things that are wrought in seasons of rest and celebration that cannot form in us any other way. There is a cost to bypassing these two; our need for productivity can rob us of holiness. We see the connection in the first part of the verse above: "Then God blessed the seventh day and made it holy, because on it He rested from all the work of creating that he had done." Rest birthed something holy. The day was *made* holy *because* He rested. And so in our efforts not to disturb productivity, we unwittingly impoverish ourselves of something far greater in value. It's no wonder there's so many stories of burnout in our world.

I believe the principle of celebration deserves its own chapter because the busyness of everyday life—especially during a succession event—can lend itself to a rush of ceaseless activity and an easy departure from celebration and "Sabbath-taking." It wouldn't surprise me if our tendency to deviate from these disciplines is the very reason why God gave Sabbath-keeping and celebration such a prominent place in Scripture, from countless references of "feasts, celebrations, and Sabbaths," even going so far as to command His people to adhere to both these disciplines. He knew how inclined many of us would be to minimize the importance of these actions and their ability to maintain balance and perspective in our lives. Our departure from celebration and rest is really only another manifestation of this recurring Eden disease of ours, another way of trying to play God by rejecting His affirmation of what is good.

We have a way of trying to prove our ability to handle everything that affects us, and this extends even to the church. Celebrating is seen as a waste of time because it keeps us from producing other things we esteem of greater value. Therein lies the tragedy: what *we* esteem of greater value. *Celebration is the remedy to this tragedy because it requires a rest from our work and a contemplation and worship of His.* It recalibrates any false estimation of what is valuable.

"Worship is the strategy by which we interrupt our preoccupation with ourselves and attend to the presence of God. Worship is the time and place that we assign for deliberate attention to God—not because he's confined to time and place but because our self-importance is so insidiously relentless that if we don't deliberately interrupt ourselves regularly, we have no chance of attending to him at all at other times and in other places."[10]

In a very small effort to reaffirm the importance of this point, I've decided to include a myriad of other voices and quotes in this chapter; it's my small way of ceasing my own writing activity and celebrating the goodness of God in the words of His people.

Celebrating allows us to be like God, while curbing those age-old tendencies attempting to become God. True God-ward celebration is—and always will be—worship. At His core, our God is a celebrating God, and He calls us to be like Him in this. Taking an extended time to celebrate this season of creation and worship the Creating God is a continuation of this Genesis rhythm that Peterson again so aptly describes: "What we're after is a seamless world of work and worship, worship and work. . . . A six-day work week concluding in worship frames the entire spirituality of creation . . ."[11]

Celebration, when engaged in a healthy way, is a great time to acknowledge the grace of God at work in us that enabled us to get this far. Most of us would agree that if someone proved integral to a major success in our life or business we would certainly take the time to honor and celebrate him or her. And yet this principle of celebration is one of the most undervalued and even altogether unobserved stages in church successions. In an action entirely unlike God, we skip right past the seventh day of creation.

Build a Corporate Altar

Throughout Scripture celebrations served to remind God's people of His goodness and ground them for the faith journey ahead. In the Old Testament the Passover feast was an annual reminder of His deliverance of the Israelites from their captivity. This rhythm of celebration and remembrance keeps God's greatness alive, resurrects the dying embers of faith that start to wane when we forget. When we skip over celebrating something God has done in our midst, we're that much closer to forgetting. When we forget who He is, we cannot help but forget who we are as a result.

From a leadership standpoint, celebration provides an opportunity to lead our congregation in building an altar of thanksgiving, grafting the memory deep within us as a community so that in future days we can recall these undeniably powerful moments that brought us to where we are. "In the Mosaic record, Sabbatism appears as a memorial of creation-work. A memorial is a monument that recalls and preserves the past; a picture that we hang up to help us keep fresh some notable event. God's Sabbatism is monumental—a remembrance—a memento. It makes creation-work memorable forever. Sabbatism is the first monument ever built . . ."[12]

We see evidence of this when Noah landed on dry ground (Gen. 8:20), when God made His promise to Abraham (Gen. 12:8). They stopped and stacked stones high and in doing so kept themselves from forgetting. It was not an afterthought for them, tacked haphazardly to the lull that often follows a major accomplishment. It was integral to determining what their future faith would be prepared to sustain! God may split a metaphorical Red Sea right at our feet, but if our faith has no altars or celebrations to recall the power of God displayed to us, will we cross? Or might a long series of missed celebrations cause our faith to suffer from an easy amnesia in moments like these? That's why it's so imperative to see the value in celebration because the monuments build upon each other, allowing our faith to grow to greater heights, individually and as a church family. Each celebratory altar built, each grafted memory of God's power and goodness paves the way for an even more robust life of faith. We connect with God, we allow our joy to be deepened by His, and as a result, we deepen.

Areas of Celebration

Now that I've spent a little time highlighting the honor that awaits you as leaders in this task of nurturing a habit of responsive celebration among your corporate body, I want to look at a few ways to do this in the specific setting of a succession event. I recognize that every church has its own unique philosophy of celebration based on the style of church and the history of its people. Due to this I'll try to steer clear of too much unnecessary detail and simply outline a broad framework of celebration that I found helpful in my journey and provide you with a short summary as to the impact.

In our church we had just three goals in our "season of celebration" that we felt were imperative. Again, the manner in which you celebrate these three areas may differ drastically but it is my recommendation that specific attention and time be given to the celebration of each area. Our three goals were to honor God by: (1) expressing thanks and appreciation to the departing senior pastor and his family,

(2) inviting the congregation to collectively celebrate God's faithfulness to us over the previous thirty-plus years, and (3) publically affirming and celebrating the new senior leader. The entire process is of grace; therefore the Lord receives all the glory.

1) Celebrating the Departing Senior Pastor

The first event was, by design, an invitational gathering because there was no way to logistically provide opportunity for the thousands of people who comprise our church family to attend a sit-down function. With the idea in mind of having about three hundred people present, the elders were extremely gracious and generous in providing a "first-class" succession celebration in a lovely, open, and inviting environment in the heart of the city. That venue, being located where it was, in the heart of the city, was symbolic as well as sensational as we had openly committed our energies and resources to be a church that cared for our city and not just the neighborhood. This venue help to reaffirm that vision in the hearts of the key leaders, longtime friends, and family members, all of whom had had an important role in the establishment and growth of our church.

Among those invited were core members, founding members, current staff and leaders, family, and close friends of the family. Individuals were given an opportunity to share stories and remembrances of particular events that had been indeed, life changing, during my season of providing leadership. The evening was a mixture of humor and emotion, from a screen show that included thirty-year-old photographs revealing just how different many of us have come to appear on the outside to the testimonies of quite a number of people who came from other cities and careers simply to add their words of celebration and remembrance of what God had done.

With all glory to God, I will never forget the deep inner joy of that experience and the unmistakable sense that we had made a statement not just about a man or one person's gifts, but rather about the power of God to change hearts, create community, and design destiny in those who trust in Him. As in the feasts and celebrations of the Old Testament, this also would serve as a bedrock of faith for those who were present who were being called to lead the community in its next season of growth in the grace of community and mission.

I clearly remember sharing with my wife, Carol, that the experience I had on that evening in the late summer of 2011 was the kind of thing that most people never get to hear because it usually is spoken at their eulogy. We felt an overwhelming amount of appreciation for our family's contribution to what God had done at North Way. What a great gift that was!

The best way to create an experience that the senior pastor really values is to have some conversation with him about the event prior to making your final plans. Let him know that "we don't need to celebrate" is not an option! Some pastors are uncomfortable when they are in the spotlight of appreciation, but as I made clear earlier, the church and the pastor need to set aside time and resources to celebrate, just as the Lord did.

Give your pastor a few options to consider. This is helpful. For example, there may be very good reasons to do something at the church. This may even be his preference. However, other options allow for some creativity and an element of the unexpected which raises everyone's anticipation.

In my case, a member of the transition team who had been tasked with the mission of finding a place for over two hundred people found a couple of conventional banquet halls that do wedding receptions, for example. Then they asked me if I would be okay with going into the heart of the city to a venue that was bright and surrounded with glass, a venue that could be configured appropriately. I loved the idea.

The main point is simply to have some honest exchanges, get comfortable with the pastor's wishes, and then use your creative gifts to make it unique and include as many as possible. It's a wonderful recognition of the history and an investment in the future of your church.

2) Celebrating Our History

The second major event took place as an all-church outdoor celebration event on a beautiful Sunday afternoon in late September. Being a multi-site church, this allowed time for the members of the church family from other locations to join us for several hours of sharing our hearts, our stories and lots of great food. I do remember leaving that event thinking that quite a number of people chose the high road rather than tell one of the many times where I had fallen on my face instead of seizing the next hill. I'm thankful for their self-control!

Once again, it's worth noting that the sharing of specific moments of breakthrough, of standing firm when circumstances seem to be pointing in other directions are very valuable lessons that need to be recalled in such times. I couldn't help but mention that the very ground where we were standing had at one time been a drive-in theater whose owner had no interest in selling to a church. In fact, it took three years of patience, three years of hearing "not interested," three years of not seeing progress until suddenly one day God came through and the deal was done.

This event also provided me with an opportunity to celebrate the gracious, wise, and joyful experience that had been made possible by the sacrifice of the transition team, Elders' Council, and all other supporting leaders. I found it nearly impossible to adequately express my appreciation for the selfless, faithful, and unusually diligent service of the transition team over the rather long process to which they had committed themselves. At North Way, it's not unusual to see volunteers go above and beyond their expected duties. However, in this major undertaking, the transition team gave themselves sacrificially and oftentimes with the difficult balance of personal preference versus long-term suitability regarding each candidate.

In celebrating our history we also wanted to spend time giving specific attention to the intricate ways God was involved in our succession process now that we were on the other side of the public transition event. There are multiple biblical instances where God's people get together to trace the history of His loving activity in their lives. The act of corporate recounting alone can foster a spirit of celebration and unity among the community. For a beautiful biblical depiction of this, see Exodus 15 for the song of Moses and Miriam after their trek across the Red Sea.

Though the succession event was the core of our celebration, we also spent a great deal of time celebrating the preceding thirty-plus years of God's favor upon North Way Christian Community. Some remarks were made, and a few lovely gifts were shared, but the main purpose of the event was to see all of the people, young and old, from all over the city, gathered together to celebrate God's goodness to us as a church family.

From my research I've found that it's common to have push-back here. Members may express concern at using church funds toward a celebration event: "This isn't the most strategic use of our time and resources." Some may bemoan that a celebration event is an "unnecessary extravagance." Celebration is not a sinful indulgence but a part of what it means to worship an extravagant God! Our redemption story should set celebration at the very core of who we are and all we do; instead, we far too often display the image mourned by Blackmur: "There are too many limp souls."[13] Please let me encourage you that if you encounter this to remember that we are created in the image of an extravagant celebrating God who calls us to extravagantly celebrate Him (Ps 103:1), not only for His good and glory, but also for ours!

As I mentioned in the opening of this chapter, I truly believe that there's something necessary and vital to this God-ordained rhythm of creation followed by rest and celebration: "Man's hallowed rest, like God's, is not to be a cessation from activity but a change of activity; not a cessation from work, but a change of work. . . . It demands from all not only a sacred pause from the humdrum of ordinary toil, but its employment in spiritual thoughts and holy pursuits."[14] As we come together to cease our "creation" work, and lead the congregation and ourselves in the work and joy of celebrating of our Creator God, there is room for a little extended extravagance here.

3) Celebrating the New Lead Pastor

The final piece of celebration for us had to do with welcoming Pastor Scott, the new lead pastor (the title that Pastor Scott preferred). The specific moment of celebration occurred at the end of the Sunday service on my final day as senior pastor. In preparing for that gathering, the transition team agreed that both the departing senior pastor and the new lead pastor would share time in the pulpit.

This was an excellent way to engage the entire church family in a moment of seeing, quite literally the transfer of authority. In order for the congregation to be able to attach a specific visual aid to that memory, here's what we did.

Perhaps the most common object that I have heard used in several locations was a simple baton like the ones used by track and field relay teams. Many weeks before the day was to occur, I already knew the exact symbol that I felt would have the most impact on Scott and the church family. I was particularly excited about this because not even the transition team knew what was planned.

Most of our congregation knows that Pastor Scott has two great loves in athletics. First, he's been a fan and participant in the age-old sport of good, old-fashioned boxing. Though a set of boxing gloves may have had more use going forward, it is Scott's other love, the hometown major-league baseball franchise known as the Pittsburgh Pirates, that provided me with a nearly perfect object illustration. I immediately saw the image of a pitcher's baseball glove that was symbolic of when a relief pitcher took over for the starter. It was in no way a perfect image as Scott wasn't coming in for an inning or two, or event to be a "closer." He was, however, coming in to relieve the starting pitcher and to continue the game in a seamless and effective way.

Probably about eight weeks prior to this transition service, I began making a connection with the Pirates organization to provide me with an authentic baseball mitt worn by one of the team's relief pitchers. The image of a healthy, strong reliever coming in to secure the win for team was on auto-replay in my mind every day leading up that service. As I finished my brief remarks that morning, I turned to the congregation and said something like, "Now please demonstrate your full support by welcoming our new lead pastor, who's coming into this position with a strong arm and heart for our mission, Pastor Scott!"

As I pulled the beautiful game-tested baseball glove out of the bag, the congregation exploded with enthusiastic applause, and I could tell that Scott not only got the image, but felt their affirmation and support as he took his new position. It was one of those rare moments that one can plan for and think about for long time, and yet it actually exceeded my expectations in terms of its impact and allowed Scott to begin his journey as leader from a position of joy and rejoicing.

As I stepped off the platform for the last time as senior pastor, I had every confidence that the Lord had directed us to identify the right man for this position at the right time. Now, over three years later, I have little doubt that anyone present then would remember a single word that was said by either of us, but nearly everyone would remember the baseball glove that Scott received as he came on to lead the team.

Here's the point. Good planning and some well-designed moments add to the celebration that is appropriate for a major achievement such as the succession of the founding or long-term senior pastor. My conviction is that the new lead (senior) pastor will provide outstanding character and leadership for the entire church family for years to come.

Moments of celebration allow us to reflect thoughtfully on the miraculous dealings of God over a specific span of time. It is the seventh day that pauses the creation work in order to allow time for the holiness of it all to sink in and deepen us. What I hope that you take away from this chapter is the sense that celebration is a beautiful and necessary interlude in the midst of the creation work of succession. It is a time of focused corporate worship, rest, and rejoicing that can introduce an even deeper holiness into the season.

There is still one more very important component to the succession process that helps ensure the longevity of all of the efforts invested thus far. It should come as no surprise that quite a few of the most difficult succession stories had their downfall several months or even years later. The new leader tried to engage his role, the people did their best to accept the differences, but doubt has a creeping way about it; words are spoken, discouragement and even division begin to subtly grow. It doesn't take long before this can result in yet another failed succession. How can we *evaluate* the health of the transition going forward? Let's examine this final but very crucial chapter that will help secure these major changes for the long-term future.

Discussion Questions for Chapter 6: Celebrate

1. Despite the undeniable fact that celebration is very much a part of the presence of God, we still find it difficult to do? Why is that?

2. On page 74, I quote Eugene Peterson, who says, "Worship is the strategy by which we interrupt the preoccupation with ourselves and attend to the presence of God." How does that expression fit into our theology of succession? Who, in fact, really is in charge of this outcome?

3. On pages 76-77, I outlined the three goals of our season of celebration. How do you resonate with what I selected and what would you do differently?

4. In the matter of bringing honor and thanks to the outgoing senior pastor, it is wise to gain an understanding of what the pastor would like to do, which may be different than what some others would prefer. Would you be comfortable having that conversation?

5. What would your response be to the few, but perhaps loud voices that are against making any expenditures just to celebrate? Why is it important for the whole church to see this very significant transition as a time for celebration?

6. The moment on transition weekend when I handed Pastor Scott the relief pitcher's baseball glove will be indelibly written on the hearts of all who witnessed it. What other kinds of visual expressions might help to seal this significant moment for your church family?

CHAPTER 7:
EVALUATE

Small Change, Big Impact

The season of evaluation is a quieter season; things are happening far underground in the very fabric of the Church body. The long-awaited fruit is almost here; it's pressing at the seams of the earth and the trees. We can smell spring in the air. Post-celebration is where we water and assess; we angle the "green things" toward the sunlight and remove anything that could hinder or harm the goal of *much fruit*. This is a season where we must remain tenacious, alert, vigilant, and prayerful.

Evaluation in the early stages of new leadership can have profound impact upon the effectiveness and productivity in days that follow. For a succession event, these beginning days for the new leader are critical in determining the momentum and longevity of all efforts and accomplishments thus far. The evaluation phase is in many ways a continuation and expansion of the integration phase, the difference being that we're now on the other side of the transition. This is where we take measures to ensure continuing success, clearing the path for loyalties to deepen as the congregation rallies around their new leader.

A different tenacity is required in the evaluation phase, one less centered upon action and more on observation and adjustment. The need here is for protection, nurture, support, and small changes. In the athletic realm sometimes all it takes to reach true greatness is the smallest shift of the wrist, or a slight change of posture. Coaches observe and evaluate the players in action, and from these insights they are able to suggest changes that can increase overall capacity and performance. One small change can take a player from good to great. That's what this stage is all about: identifying places in need of change or additional support so that the church and leadership can reach its full potential.

To return to my earlier analogy in the book, the heart has been transplanted, and we have witnessed the very sacred moment where life-giving blood surges through the veins to the rest of the body. Even though the body may show signs of initial functionality with the new heart, there still exists a measure of fragility and possible regression, especially in these beginning days. The fact that the new heart is beating is wonderful and worthy of deep celebration, but it is not a valid measure of certain or continued success—that is determined by careful observation and attention in the weeks and months ahead.

In the medical world a transplant patient will undergo an intensive after-care program of recovery, often involving time in a protected environment to stave off infection and lessen the risk of organ rejection. The new heart, in fact the whole body, needs a period of time to restore and heal. In this season of evaluation, we would be wise to mirror the medical approach and exert great care and attention to watching for the slightest signs of infection and committing to react immediately if we see any red flags developing. The success of the transplant and succession is hinged both on the preparation before the transplant *and* the after-care efforts to support full acceptance. Evaluation is where we tend to the deep-rooted grafting. Our efforts here will do wonders in determining the future productivity and fruitfulness of the Church or organization.

Freshman Year

Most honeymoons are followed by a wonderful (albeit less glamorous) adjustment period. In my opinion, the months following the succession event should absolutely still be considered part of the overall succession process. These are strategic months. These are the months where patterns form, expectation are set, and rhythms are adopted that will either work to compromise or solidify the preceding work. You don't get this opportunity back again. A succession, like a child, only goes through this formative stage once. After the honeymoon is where we discover whether or not he takes out the trash without being asked, or if she leaves the toothpaste cap off, or just how many days they can peacefully coexist with the in-laws in town. This is where the gritty, glorious, day-to-day process of redemption and growth begins. The moment of the long-awaited succession announcement is climatic, but the real growth and depth of a marriage is not forged at the ceremony, but in the days thereafter.

The transition team and the Elders' Council coined the phrase "freshman year" to describe the first twelve months of Scott's new leadership. This term helped to provide some mental grace from the beginning. As any innovative leader or executive will tell you, in order for creativity and vision to have space to develop, there must also be room for error and readjustment. The succession experience was brand new to all of us. Grace was a necessary starting point in every interaction.

The term "freshman year" also helped remind us to tread carefully with any changes during this beginning season. It will take anywhere from three to six months for the church to begin to adjust to a new leader, let alone any new strategic plans or programming. Even though the new pastor may come with a significant number of ideas that everyone believes will be well received by the congregation, *now is not the time to initiate deep change or undergo any major adjustments*. Even though a fully healthy heart may be transplanted into the body, the patient is not prepared to leave the recovery room and run a marathon later that afternoon. Seams need to heal, trust needs to be established between the pastor and congregation. Freshman year is a time to let the dust settle, let things solidify, and allow the natural healing and recovery process to run its course.

Certainly small changes can be made to help the new leadership team to be more effective. My best counsel is to wait at least six months before you even consider introducing significant changes in how you conduct worship, or a discipleship strategy, or anything that involves or impacts the church as a whole. It's easy to underestimate the amount of time required for the church to embrace the changes in the staff you have just introduced. As I recall, the strategy our pastoral team and elders took was to simply do what was already in place more effectively the entire freshman year.

Logistics

It seems important to underscore that the task of evaluation was intended to assess both the numerical and relational components involved. We wanted to keep an eye on our progress, identify potential problems or places of regression, and make sure that everyone involved remained spiritually healthy and encouraged.

There were a few specific areas of evaluation that we focused on, including how Pastor Scott was being received by the elders and staff, how the other three candidates who were not selected were readjusting to the campus or position they were assigned, and how the relationship between the former senior pastor and the new lead pastor was developing.

The other campus pastors who had gone through the rigorous interview/investigation process returned to their previous assignments with notable humility and open enthusiasm about the final outcome. We have all changed as a result of the season of succession, and we have all grown remarkably through this extended time of prayer, analysis, and profound hunger to see the will of God fulfilled in our church.

As is our practice, any members of the church could speak with an elder on any weekend and share perspectives, questions, or concerns regarding ministry. This is crucial for any ministry that desires to be transparent and even more so during a time of major change. These concerns and feedback that may arise from the congregation are a wonderful form of evaluation all on their own and can provide excellent fodder for discussion and to highlight places in need of adjustment or attention. It's with great awareness of the grace of God that we can share that well over three years have passed and we remain one in spirit.

In some church cultures it is the norm for the departing pastor to actually depart. In our situation we didn't believe that this was necessary for the health of for the health of the team or the new senior leader. In fact, it was just the opposite: I was welcomed to stay on board as a member of the pastoral team going into the future! My role was to stay engaged in certain aspects of the ministry while giving full and unconditional support to Pastor Scott's leadership. I know that this is a rare situation and possibly even a rare perspective, but it is one that our people greatly valued and one that I believe strengthened the succession event as a whole. In a culture where people jump from one commitment to another, one coast to another, one social media outlet to another; the idea of an abiding, relationally consistent, and kingdom-driven vision is extremely appealing. It becomes the rock, the anchor upon which significant commitments are made. For those who had a long history with North Way, this brought reassurance that we were holding to our core values and commitments even though certain elements of style or even priorities might change in the upcoming months and years. For people that were new to our church, it gave them a profound sense of the deep foundation that had been laid over the previous thirty years and spoke volumes to the stability of this congregation that they were considering as their possible home church. If anything, I believe this enabled and possibly even expedited the congregation to embrace Scott's leadership with even more trust and appreciation.

This allowed the process of evaluation to be seamless in the sense that Scott and I were both intently monitoring the health of the church from both of our unique positions, and we were simultaneously able to support each other as our roles were new to both of us. We knew that we had a better chance together of recognizing any issues that might need addressing, personally or corporately.

It's my greatest encouragement for this evaluation stage that, if the situation allows, the pastor is asked to stay on in a position of mentor and support for the new leader. If he is not able to do this locally, then some form of phone or email accountability and mentoring should be established. The departing pastor is the person most able to give insight to the new leader because he has intimately experienced the inner workings of the ministry and people now under the responsibility of the new leader.

I'm guessing that all of us have heard at least one horror story involving a pastor who has not left his church or community and has remained close enough to what is going on the church that the people never really embrace the new leader, but simply look at the signals of the now departed senior pastor to see if he agrees with what's going on.

Just as it is in the medical world, there are some forms of affliction that can only be stopped by amputation. If the departing senior pastor is unable to release his or her positional authority, then amputation is probably the only alternative. However, let's be very clear that it has been self-inflicted. We are proof that this relationship can result in health and encouragement while both pastors remain involved both in the local church and the greater community at large. It's an incredible statement of Christians loving each other through change rather than divorcing each other. I am in no way promising that this is easy, but it is very possible by the grace of God and in fact, I would say, incredibly rewarding to see the ministry not just continue on, but flourish under new leadership. Just as a good parent richly celebrates and finds joy in the accomplishments of his or her child, so it is with celebrating the growth of a beloved Church family under new leadership.

When you strip things down to the bare walls, all that this relationship really requires of the departing pastor is his willingness to neither be engaged in the daily decision-making processes, nor offer opinions about the decisions that are made for any reason unless input is specifically requested.

This may seem like a small thing, but during the season after the initial transfer of authority, it is very easy for the leadership of the new pastor to be undermined. The congregation is accustomed to following the departing leader, and if the former leader continues to lead or communicate from a position of authority—especially in any matter that contradicts the new leader—it will put the church members in an impossible situation, ultimately forcing them to divide their loyalty and most likely leading to a church split. The chances of survival or growth of any kind in this atmosphere are slim to none. Just imagine if the surgeon decided that instead of removing the old heart he'd instead transplant the new one right alongside it. As the old saying goes, "Anything with two heads is a monster." Nobody is capable of supporting two hearts. In order for a transplant to work the old heart must be removed from functioning at the core of the body.

If you're in a situation where the senior pastor has been asked to leave, or by some other determination has been required to leave, then there's a significant need for someone with tenure and integrity to be communicating with the new senior or lead pastor. In my experience, most churches would not look outside of their own leadership for assistance or help even in difficult times. Therefore, it would make sense to empower the most respected and longest tenured elders to provide the basis of communication and assistance for the new pastor to be assimilated into the church culture. It would also make sense that a select leader or two from the transition team would also be a great support during these very important months.

I realize that this is an unusual suggestion and thought it might be beneficial to share a bit of how The Elders' Council and transition team worked attentively with me to create a new position that had meaningful responsibility, yet no longer carried spiritual authority in matters of church leadership. We titled my role as that of "Founding Pastor." I was assigned a number of specific duties but the only person to whom I had to report was Pastor Scott. This made for a very healthy accountability but not through a long chain of command. This has worked very well for both of us.

I was given significant responsibility to complete the establishment of the extension campus of the Trinity Evangelical Divinity School that was formed over the previous five years of my leadership role. This was a wonderful assignment because it gave me opportunity to interface with other churches and universities who were looking for graduate-level learning possibilities in our area. They also gave me responsibility to continue to encourage the engagement of over one hundred North Way volunteers who served an inner-city school as tutors, mentors, coaches, and friends. The team also encouraged me to meet with various pastors to discuss, share, and encourage them in matters of personal and relational growth, not so much in terms of the strategic ministry responsibilities. As most every pastor will tell you, it is very often at the personal level the pastors feel the greatest pressure from their strategic and pastoral responsibilities. This responsibility also was a wonderful place for me to continue affirming my support of Scott as these were the members that would be affected by the change in leadership in more day-to-day experiences.

As I alluded to above, I also viewed this role of founding pastor as an opportunity to continue the integration tasks on this side of the transition. It's probably worth noting that on every occasion that I had an opportunity to publicly affirm Pastor Scott, I did so with authentic enthusiasm. Likewise, there are meaningful statements by Pastor Scott about the foundation that was laid in the previous thirty years, as well as our current relationship that continues to thrive. Small things like personal home meetings (see page 50) or just showing up at a missions board or counseling center meeting gave a strong message of continuity and support.

Critical to all of this public affirmation was a weekly one-on-one, face-to-face meeting that Scott and I had with each other. That sixty-to-ninety-minute private sit-down time allowed us to share our hearts with each other, discuss complex issues from a long-term perspective as well as the newer one, and seek agreement on decisions that had significant implications. For example, one of the areas where Scott needed clarity was in determining how much he should be involved in other events around the city where we (our church) were expected to show up but had little connection with our own specific mission. We were able to be sounding boards for one another as we determined together what was and was not of great strategic importance and what could easily become a peripheral distraction.

Best of all, those private times together served as a weekly reminder that we had made a commitment to have each other's back, no matter what. With that posture, outside criticism and internal rumors had little, if any, traction to gain.

On the flip side of things, every month or so I received a call from one of the Elders' Council members to get together for coffee to simply listen to one another. These very casual but sincere and authentic connections let me know with deep certainty that these men really cared how my wife and I were handling these totally new feelings in this season of our faith journey. I cannot tell you how affirming those follow-up meetings were. Having journeyed through the succession process in the role of former/founding pastor,

I would deeply encourage you to be intentional in following up with the former leader.

On a personal note, I have discovered that many who reach this phase in their life with no particular responsibility on their plates very often become disillusioned or even depressed because of the absence of the challenges and opportunities. In many ways, allowing the departing pastor to remain in a mentor role not only benefits the new senior pastor but the departing pastor as well. The transition was seamless for me because I was given the opportunity to continue to provide leadership in several key areas of our church's mission while being free to pursue other things in a much less structured schedule. I cannot overstate my appreciation to our elders for such a gracious and generous transition opportunity. This is how it should be done, and they did it *extremely* well.

As the church family observed us thriving in this new season in our lives, it simply confirmed to them that the new leadership team was doing an excellent job fulfilling the mission to which they had been called. I can honestly say that I did not have a single contact asking me if I thought the new leadership was on the right track. Our people could tell that there was unity, respect, and mutual edification behind the scenes as well as in times of worship gatherings and meetings. It did not take long for this to result in measurable parameters of weekend attendance, weekly giving, and small group and ministry participation. In each of these key areas there was an eight-to-ten percent annual growth rate. One could just sense the joy and excitement of the new chapters that were about to unfold.

Identify Red Flags

In the opening I alluded to red flags that can pop up in these early months. I want to spend a little time addressing what to do when evaluation uncovers issues needing less of a preventative and more of a restorative approach. There will be times when, despite our very best efforts, things do not develop as we had planned and prayed. Typically it won't take long for warning signs to surface, red flags serving as early indicators that something isn't right. The warning signs, like a fever, are symptoms alerting us to the fact that something deeper is wrong, something that will not improve without attention. The fever is not what needs addressing but the infection causing the fever. As the failure rate of successions indicate, infection can spread fast and have devastating results. Establishing evaluation as a priority allows us to recognize problem areas right at the beginning, and by committing to address the root of any issues that arise (instead of just a quick, topical fix), we protect the overall integrity of the succession.

While the list below is by no means exhaustive, it does contain some common red flags and indicates that action is required on the part of the elders or overall highest authority in the church:

- Core members or volunteer leaders ask for personal meetings to discuss issues they are facing within their ministries.
- Spontaneous prayer meetings that pop up because of concern for the church's direction (especially ones not involving the new lead pastor).
- Elders or deacons begin to be absent from regular meetings.
- Staff members come to the elders or other church members to express concerns.
- Rapid changes or restructuring of personnel, programming, ministries, or budget.
- The trend of dropping attendance and most especially a significant drop in regular giving would be a clear signal that the succession may be in peril as it suggests that the relational and financial support of the congregation is deteriorating.

All of these indicators do not mean that the succession process is doomed; they simply highlight a specific area in need of correction and additional support and communication moving forward. The need to readjust does not suggest failure on the part of the transition team, departing leader, or new leader. It simply attests to the fact that the changes involving a major leadership shift are multi-faceted and relationally complex and require a bit of honing for all the new pieces to fit together well.

I would encourage you to keep the prayer team engaged and informed throughout this freshman year, perhaps even giving them specific areas to pray for that address the distinct adjustments required of the new and departing pastor, leadership, staff, volunteers, and congregation. Prayers for the unyielding support and positive response of the congregation to the new leader go a long way to covering the upcoming days with protection and peace. And as you pray for those who stay, pray also for those who will depart. No matter who is selected, or how perfectly the succession process is navigated, there will be some who are unable or unwilling to support the new leader/direction, especially in larger congregations. We try to enable these people to transition elsewhere without damaging any relational bonds. Learn to bless them as they go elsewhere and not allow them to drain you of energy and focus that might overshadow the exciting things that are happening. Finally, pray that many new people will be drawn to the church as a result of the renewed excitement of the congregation.

We are well over three years since the formal transition service took place. Recognizing that a healthy ministry is one that continues to grow and reproduce disciples, it is a great joy to report that North Way has grown in every measurable statistical way. At the three year mark since the leadership transition, the overall church worship attendance has grown over fifteen percent, and our financial support has grown proportionally. The sense that God's favor and blessing remains upon us is truly humbling and praiseworthy.

For our church, we have now come to the place where the new senior leader is able to fashion the next phase of the church vision. Whereas the first months or even years following the succession were focused on galvanizing the church and acting on already existing plans, things have progressed to where we stand ready to move ahead. In fact, by the grace of God and very intentional prayer and humility, we have found our new rhythm and are celebrating the successful launch of our fifth campus two-and-a-half years after the actual succession event. It's with great humility and a sense of the providence of God and appreciation for the grace that's been shared among fellow elders and pastors that we can report that life at North Way continues to grow.

The task of evaluation, though still of great value, is not as central to our attention as it once was. As time passes, health will increase, and the risks involved with succession will decrease. Just as with an organ transplant patient, the need for doctor visits/evaluation will becomes less frequent until perhaps the only thing needed is an annual health check-up. Those most intimately connected with the details of the transition will feel when this shifts. Things will move from monitoring and strengthening to mobilizing. Slowly but surely the effort required to graft in the new leader and changes will lessen, and a new rhythm will develop all on its own. The goal of a succession or major transition event is that the body will reach even greater health than was previously possible. The legacy of this is one of growth, life, expansion. The goal is to be more, not less, as a result of this process. Evaluation can help expedite the time it takes to reach the season of fruitfulness that naturally follows a successful transition.

Discussion Questions for Chapter 7: Evaluate

1. Why is it that quite a number of church successions fail after all of these other steps might've been taken? Why are we vulnerable in this next season?
2. It's my opinion that we let our guard down because we have traveled on a long and arduous journey to get here. What can we do to see that this transition will flourish?
3. Read pages 85-87 once again and discuss the concept of the "freshman year" of rather intensive ongoing evaluations and adjustments in order for the change to become deeply rooted. What specific steps would you add to what we proposed?
4. If other pastors from within your church were considered but not selected, this is a very important time to reaffirm their vital role and calling to the position that they hold. What else might you do to continue to nurture these strong leaders and not lose them to an unknown hurt or oversight?
5. Why do so many churches find it necessary to ask the departing senior pastor to worship elsewhere? What is the essential posture for the pastor to take in order to continue to not only worship at his church but possibly even continue to serve? (p. 89)
6. In this chapter, I make the point that the personal connections with individual elders and couples as well as members of the

pastoral team serve to affirm our role in this new season. Is this something that your church would embrace?

7. Finally, look back over this entire process. Did you sense the favor of God? Did you actually grow through all of this? If so, how might you share this joy with others?

CONCLUSION

I mentioned in the beginning that my hope in writing this book is that these words would do a fierce and glorious job at counteracting and preventing this infection of failed successions from occurring in the lives and ministries of those who read it. And in the cases of already failed attempts, I pray that it would work to heal that which has been disappointed and damaged, restoring hope and faith enough for future transitions.

I tried to take great care not to minimize the gravity of succession; I would be a fool to disregard the statistics. But I also cannot state enough what a great loss can happen to those who rush blindly past this significant invitation from our good God to participate in His work and enter into His joy. Succession has the potential to propel a church into a season that is truly magnificent. Isn't this often where true greatness lies, caught in the balance between daunting earthly statistics and the relentless love and efforts of God to build His Church, especially when all odds are stacked against us? In all the stories—Gideon in battle, the falling of Jericho, the escape from Egypt—the odds of their success were laughable, and yet God was on their side. The same is true here. The odds are stacked high, but *God is here*. It's the way of paradox. The least are the greatest, the poorest have the most, and the most powerful appear to be powerless. So it is with succession. What many expect to cause significant upheaval can, by the grace of God, incite greater unity and effectiveness within the Kingdom. It can be, indeed, a *seamless succession*.

The principles in these pages are intended to help sustain momentum, productivity, and growth through the succession event, calling us always to lift our head up high to the one who is our

Helper. My prayers, hope, and faith journey with you in the upcoming changes; may joy accompany you in each and every stage:

- **Initiate** the succession planning with tenacity, prayer, expectation, and *hope.*
- **Cultivate** a climate prepared and willing to support and celebrate the changes surrounding succession.
- **Communicate** information in such a way that serves to prepare those who this change will most impact.
- **Investigate** options for the future senior leader based upon assessed church needs and a corresponding position description, starting first with in-house candidates and broadening the search, if necessary
- **Integrate** the selected leader into his new role through information and affirmation.
- **Celebrate** the goodness of God as a community, giving specific attention to the service of the outgoing leader and the incoming leader.
- **Evaluate** places in need of additional support and adjustment in the early days to expedite the journey towards productivity and fruitfulness.

In these closing pages I want to be sensitive in addressing the possibility that you may do everything right and yet things still fall apart at the end. Perhaps this has already been your story. There are times when even our most valiant of efforts fail. The gravity of this fallen world can be hard to counteract. People may disappoint us in this process; we may disappoint ourselves. The new leader may underestimate the effort required and abruptly leave after only a few weeks or months. Relational complications may impede the momentum of the transition team or even dissolve it altogether. As I willingly admitted in the opening and throughout these pages, I did not navigate this change perfectly. It is impossible to navigate this change perfectly because it involves imperfect people. These principles are not fail-safe, but I do wholeheartedly believe that they will provide significant assistance in carving out a grace-filled, Spirit-led, well-informed approach from which to pursue a season of succession that results in our collective victory, and His glory. I do believe that there is grace enough for this process to position a church for greatness instead of decay, life instead of loss—and in the cases of failed attempts, redemption and recovery instead of ruin. Because of the goodness of God, the efforts of His people, and the principles in these pages, I have witnessed this grace, this growth, this joy.

In fact, my experience of the succession process was so positive that I put together a small, but very experienced core group of men and women who share this same passion and burden. Having experienced the succession process first-hand, we would be delighted to pursue a conversation with you, journey in faith, and hope beside you as you seek to make this change effectively, regardless of your demographic, size, or denominational affiliation. Please check out the Passavant Leadership Group website for more details.

Finally, if you have feedback or questions with reference to this book, I would count it a privilege to engage in conversation with you. Just go to our website and follow the simple guidelines there to connect with us. My prayer is that we will all continue to receive abundant grace during these times of major transition and our goal of a *seamless succession*.

We welcome your inquiries or input at SeamlessSuccession@ passavantlg.com or www.passavantleadershipgroup.com.

ACKNOWLEDGEMENTS

There are so many individual people for whom I want to express my deep affection and appreciation. This has never been a ministry built by or upon the strengths of one individual.

With that in mind, it seemed appropriate to me to acknowledge two very important sources that helped shape the essence of this book.

The first is J. J. Cozzens who served as my writing coach and organizational advisor on this project. J.J.'s considerable experience in the art of writing was of great help and encouragement to me throughout this process. Thank you, my friend!

The other is a corporate source, the friends and colleagues who comprise our pastoral team and especially the transition team, whom I mentioned numerous times in the body of the work. When the reader sees the pronoun "we," it's almost always in reference to these dedicated and gifted members of the group that was charged with overseeing the entire succession process. Thank you for your devotion, sacrifice, and faithfulness.

About Passavant Leadership Group

P LG has helped to provide primary oversight and leadership in the successful transition of a 4,000 member church from its Founding Pastor to a widely affirmed and accepted successor who has developed a team that has released the church to even greater growth and fruitfulness.

Our leadership has also helped in the transition of a stagnant, older congregation of 200 into a vital, younger church of 1500 in weekly attendance.

We have a wealth of experience in working with much smaller churches in urban, suburban and even rural settings. We understand that every church is called by God, regardless of its size or location, and is placed there to become an agent of life-change and transformation by the power of the Holy Spirit.

"Leadership succession is one of the most important issues facing the Church today, and Jay Passavant lays out not only his story of successful succession, but also key steps and practical application on how you can effectively hand off, pass the baton, and even take the baton into the future. Effective, practical, and inspirational."
- Brad Lomenick
Best Selling Author, The Catalyst Leader

"Jay Passavant did something that few pastors do well."
- Jim Tomberlin
Founder and Senior Strategist, MultiSite Solutions

"I am certain that PLG will help you in whatever season of ministry you are currently serving."
- John Nuzzo
Senior Pastor, Victory Family Church, Cranberry Twp., PA

"[PLG] is championing the good things that God is doing in and through us."
- Rick Rufenacht
Senior Pastor, First Church of God, Defiance, OH

Contact us at: **www.passavantleadershipgroup.com**
800-514-1986

NOTES

Introduction

1. William Vanderbloemen and Warren Bird, *Next: Pastoral Succession That Works*, (Michigan: BakerBooks, 2014), 12.
2. John Kotter, "Leading Change: Why Transformational Efforts Fail" in *Harvard Business Reviews 10 Must Reads: On Change*, (Massachusetts: Harvard Business Review Press, 2011), 5.

Chapter 1

3. Robert E. Quinn, *Deep Change: Discovering the Leader Within*, (San Francisco: The Jossey-Bass Business & Management Series, 1996).
4. Paul Billheimer, *Destined for the Throne*, (Minneapolis: Bethany House Publishers and Fort Washington, PA: Christian Literature Crusade, 1975), 131.
5. Billheimer, *Destined for the Throne*, 102.
6. Billheimer, *Destined for the Throne*, 102.

Chapter 2

7. Dictionary.com, March 2015, https://www.dictionary.com/browse/cultivate?s=t

Chapter 3

8. John P. Kotter and Dan S. Cohen, preface to: *The Heart of Change*, (Massachusetts: Harvard Business School Press, 2002), x.
9. Mike Myatt, "The #1 Reason CEO Successions Fail", *CEO. com*, August 8, 2012,

http://www.ceo.com/business_and_government/
the-1-reason-ceo-successions-fail/

Chapter 6

10. Euguene Peterson, *Leap Over a Wall: Earthy Spirituality for Everyday Christians*, (New York: HarperCollins, 1997), 152-153.
11. Peterson, *Leap Over a Wall*, 27.
12. S. H. Nesbit, *The Sabbath of the Bible*, (Pittsburgh: Myers, Shinkle & Co, 1890), 15.
13. R.P. Blackmur, *Henry Adams*, (New York: Harcourt Branch Jovanavich, 1980), 73.
14. Nesbit, *Sabbath of the Bible*, 41-42.

CPSIA information can be obtained at www.ICGtesting.com
Printed in the USA
BVOW02s2054290715

410890BV00002B/200/P